English as a Second Language: Dimensions and Directions

English as a Second Language: Dimensions and Directions

Irwin Feigenbaum
Editor

A Publication of
The Summer Institute of Linguistics
and
The University of Texas at Arlington

1984

© 1984 by the Summer Institute of Linguistics
Library of Congress Catalog Card No.:83-051796
ISBN 0-88312-929-9

Copies of this and other publications of the Summer Institute of Linguistics may be obtained from:

Summer Institute of Linguistics
Department of Academic Publications
7500 W. Camp Wisdom Road
Dallas, TX 75236

Contents

Foreword vii

A Critical Evaluation of Some New ESL Methods 1
        Thomas Scovel

Language Testing: Where to from Here? 15
        John W. Oller, Jr.

Applied Linguistics: The Use of Linguistics in ESL   47
        Christina Bratt Paulston

Foreword

Each semester of the academic year, the Department of Foreign Languages and Linguistics at the University of Texas at Arlington and the International Linguistics Center of the Summer Institute of Linguistics sponsor the Linguistics Forum Series--a series of lectures, papers, or other presentations dealing with one area of linguistics or applied linguistics. In the fall of 1982 the topic was "English as a Second or Foreign Language: Dimensions and Directions."

This topic was especially timely, both for the field of English as a second or foreign language and for our new program at UTA. Recently, the field of ES/FL has expanded in a number of different directions. New linguistic models and new pedagogical approaches have proliferated. The EFL program we have established at UTA has involved introducing teacher-preparation course-work and structuring classes for non-native speakers of English--both credit and intensive classes. In establishing our program, we have had to ask a number of questions to which the answers are not obvious. For example, which methodologies should be presented in teacher-training courses? Which should be incorporated in our English-language classes? The proliferation of new points of view in the field has meant that it is not easy to bring together the information on which to base our answers. Therefore, it seemed worthwhile to take stock of the field of ES/FL. In the fall of 1982, the Linguistics Forum Series was directed toward assisting in this state-of-the-field assessment.

The four lectures were planned in the following way:

1. Important areas of research and experimentation were selected (structure of English, methodology, testing, and linguistics).

2. Three questions were proposed:
   a. In the past, what information from the area has been especially useful in the field of ES/FL?
   b. What is the present state of the area insofar as it contributes to the field?
   c. What are fruitful directions for future research and investigation which will be applicable in the field?
3. Authorities in the areas were invited to answer the questions.

The Fall 1982 Linguistics Forum Series

September	Sidney Greenbaum University of Wisconsin-Milwaukee	"English Grammar and ESL"
October	Thomas Scovel San Francisco State University	"A Critical Evaluation of Some New ESL Methods"
November	John W. Oller, Jr. University of New Mexico	"Language Testing: Where To From Here?"
December	Christina Bratt Paulston University of Pittsburgh	"Applied Linguistics: The Use of Linguistics in ESL"

This volume includes three of the four presentations. (Greenbaum's will appear in G. Nickel and J. Stalker (eds.), <u>IRAL</u>, Special Issue, forthcoming.)

<u>Language Teaching Methodology</u>

In the late 1960's and in the 1970's, new methodologies sprang up in many parts of the field of foreign language pedagogy. These methodologies now rain down on experienced teacher and new-comer, with promises of outstanding results, but these new methods have arisen from different backgrounds and are constructed on different bases. Therefore, a classroom teacher or a program director is hard-pressed to make an informed decision about which method(s) to use.

Scovel compares eight contemporary foreign language teaching methodologies; he uses six questions as

Foreword

the basis of this comparison. These questions help us to see more clearly the ways in which methods are similar and dissimilar, aside from the great differences that often appear at first sight. The answers to the questions yield descriptions of these methodologies; in addition, they indicate the dimensions of current experimentation.

Scovel's method of characterizing methodologies is also valuable in itself; we can apply his questions to any methodology. Since students have different goals in learning English, we cannot prescribe one method for all classes or even for all students in one class. Rather, with greater insight into what we do and how we do it, we are in a better position to improve the effectiveness of our teaching in any given context. And with a clearer understanding of the dimensions of teaching methodologies, we are better able to introduce real innovation--not just apparent differences--into our future work.

Language Testing

What does it mean to say that someone speaks English (or any other language--native or foreign)? The answer to this question is very complex, but despite that, it is important because it will inform our second- or foreign-language pedagogy: we want to ensure that students learn what they must know in order to speak English. And of course, we want to test their mastery of this material.

Oller recognizes the intimate interconnection between the fields of language teaching and language testing; and in assessing one field, he deals with both. The history of foreign language testing and teaching reflects the evolution of ideas about language structure and use. Although previous ideas continue, Oller looks forward to a trend he calls "pragmatic-textual." Since language is not just a list of items (phones, words, sentence patterns, etc.), teaching and testing should take into account that language is found in texts. When the logic of a text is not observed, that text is difficult to understand.

There are important implications of this text view of language for the field of second- and foreign-language pedagogy: language learning should be presented in real-life contexts; we should use texts that describe motivated activities; texts should deal with action that can be staged; and we should respect people's life experience, which is logical.

Applied Linguistics

The three questions proposed for each area (its past, present, and future) presuppose the existence of information contributing to the field of ES/FL. In her discussion of the "use of linguistics in ESL," Paulston starts at a more fundamental level. First, she asks whether linguistics can be applied in the field. Then if the answer is affirmative, how can it be applied? The second question entails the kind of information needed for this application.

Paulston does not approach the questions as many linguists and teacher trainers do, with the assumption that the utility of linguistics is obvious; instead, she goes to potential users of linguistic information --classroom teachers--in order to find out what is actually used. She observes them and discusses their teaching with them.

The use of linguistics in the field of ES/FL has not been unidirectional, either in chronology or in cause-and-effect: the theory has not been first developed and then later applied. The field has benefitted from insights from diverse sources. They include different linguistic models, but equally important are the "complex" fields like sociolinguistics, where linguistics interacts with other fields, with the result of this interaction then applied to the foreign-language context.

In recent years, information has come to the field of ES/FL from many directions. How can it be applied? Paulston's conclusion is that the application is not always apparent or direct; nevertheless, it is important. It influences teaching, partly through the knowledge that teachers have and partly through the different attitudes that teachers have toward language.

A time of heterodoxy, as we now have in ES/FL, produces benefits in the large amounts of information developed and contributed by other fields. However, quantity is not a necessary indication of quality, and we can be overcome by the weight of the contributions. That is why a periodic "stock-taking" is worthwhile. These papers were intended for this purpose. The authors help us to see order and direction in large amounts of information through their appreciation of the impact of other areas on the field of English as a second or foreign language.

Irwin Feigenbaum

A Critical Evaluation of Some New ESL Methods*

Thomas Scovel

San Francisco State University

Introduction

The field of teaching English has grown enormously over the past two decades, both in terms of numbers of students and teachers, as well as in regard to the variety of materials and methods employed. Having taught in the Peoples Republic of China a few years ago, and having become acquainted with some of the EFL programs in the world's most populous nation, I have direct knowledge of this tremendous growth. One of the most dramatic transformations which has taken place has been in the area of foreign language methodology. Because many of these newer methods are still not widely publicized nor clearly understood, I thought it might be instructive if I were to share with you in this Linguistics Forum Series, a personal description and appraisal of six of these new approaches, describing them concisely, and then concluding with a few, brief practical criticisms. The six methods which I wish to review fall into three categories: 1) Delayed Oral Production Methods: the Postovsky Method and the Asher Method; 2) Innovative Audio-Lingual Methods: the Rassias Method and the Thomas Method; and 3) Interpersonal Methods: the Silent Way and Community Language Learning.

Before I introduce these novel approaches, let me briefly review the salient characteristics of the two most popular traditional methods--methods with which all of you are intimately acquainted. These two old

---

*This is a revised version of an article entitled "Six New Methods for Teaching Foreign Languages from the United States," to appear in Zielsprache Englisch.

standbys are the Direct Method and the Grammar-Translation Method. Time and tide may wait for no man, but they certainly pause for these two approaches: like Old Man River, they seem to just keep on rolling along. Referring to the table on the following page, which classifies these two traditional methods along with the six new ones which are the focus of my discussion, you will note that the first question--Does the teacher rely almost exclusively on the L_2?--pertains most directly to the Direct Method. The hallmark of this method is the almost exclusive use of the target language in the classroom. Examples of the Direct Method are found in commercial language teaching enterprises such as Berlitz and Inlingua, but the heavy reliance on the language to be learned is a technique popular in many different language teaching methodologies. This is exemplified by the YES cells in the first row of the Table.

The second question pertains most appropriately to the Grammar-Translation Method, because this is an approach that has traditionally been concerned with the teaching of structure. The Grammar-Translation approach has always been associated with a heavy emphasis on grammatical patterns and morphological paradigms, with a great deal of attention given to the correct identification and classification of Latinate terms and parts of speech. Part of this fascination with grammatical detail can be traced to a tradition of Medieval scholasticism, where instead of asking how many angels could dance on the head of a pin, young grammarians were queried about the number of gerunds or participles that could pirouette at the end of a clause. The historical evolution of the Grammar-Translation Method, as well as many of the approaches and techniques which we believe to be quite modern, is well documented by L. G. Kelly (1969). I will not discuss either of these traditional methods further; they are introduced here mainly as a foil against which we can place the half-dozen new approaches which deserve our consideration, contemplation, and criticism.

It is important to realize, of course, that there are a great many new methods which have been developed. Lozanov's Suggestopedia, which I have thoroughly reviewed elsewhere (Scovel 1979), is a well-publicized approach to foreign language pedagogy that I have not included in this present survey. Another point worth mentioning is that these methods are not restricted to the teaching of the foreign language for which they were originally developed. In this respect, teachers of

Comparison of Some Foreign Language Teaching Methodologies

	Traditional Methods		Delayed Prod	Oral Methods	Innovative AL Methods		Interpersonal Methods	
	D M	G T	Post	Asher	Rass	Thom	S W	C L L
1. Does the teacher rely almost exclusively on the L2?	YES	NO	YES	YES	NO	NO	YES	NO
2. Is there heavy emphasis on teaching ling structures?	NO	YES	YES	NO	YES	YES	YES	NO
3. Is there a conscious attempt to delay speaking skills?	NO	NO	YES	YES	NO	NO	NO	NO
4. Is there a great deal of physical activity in class?	NO	NO	NO	YES	YES	NO	NO	NO
5. Is there primary emphasis on interpersonal factors?	NO	NO	NO	NO	NO	NO	YES	YES
6. Does the student have strong influence on the curriculum?	NO	NO	NO	NO	NO	NO	NO	YES

The methods cited are D M, the Direct Method; G T , Grammar Translation; Post, the Postovsky Method; Asher, the Total Physical Response; Rass, the Rassias or "Dartmouth" Method; Thom, the Michel Thomas Method; S W, the Silent Way (Gattegno); C L L, Community Language Learning (Curran)

Spanish, French, and German can learn from those of us working in ESL, and, of course, many of the innovations which were originally designed for ESL students are applicable to the instruction of any other modern language. Most of the new methods reviewed here were first developed to teach a language other than English (e.g., Postovsky first used his method for Russian and Rassias for French); nevertheless, all have been adopted for the teaching of ESL. It should also be pointed out that there is a great deal of continuity between these "new" methods and the traditional methods used in the past. Indeed, the first four methods I shall review are essentially renovated forms of the old Audio-Lingual Method (AL) popularized by Charles Fries thirty-five years ago. Finally, although it is my task to describe the differences among the methods under review, this goal should not obscure the fact that there are many characteristics common to all good methods. The differences that do exist are usually those of priorities and emphasis rather than of pedagogical goals.

Delayed Oral Production Methods

The salient characteristic of these methods is the seriousness with which they subscribe to the AL dictum on skill sequencing, "listening before speaking." Using largely their perception of how children acquire a mother tongue under natural circumstances, the proponents of these methods argue that adult (or child) second language learning should replicate first language acquisition, and it is vitally important to have a period of time when the foreign language learner can simply absorb the sounds and structures of the new language without being forced to worry about pronunciation and production. According to the proponents of this type of pedagogical approach, experiments with foreign language learners have demonstrated the efficiency and efficacy of these methods (Gary and Gary 1980; Postovsky 1974; and Winitz 1981). Furthermore, some of these methodologists cite support for their emphasis on delaying any spoken communication in the target language from the popular second language acquisition "monitor" model proposed by Stephen Krashen--the contention is that by allowing for a period of nonspeaking "intake", the second language learner can "acquire" the target language naturally, rather than "learn" it in a conscious and somewhat unnatural manner (Asher 1979).

What does the classroom teacher actually do to achieve this goal of delaying speech production, and, more importantly, what kind of feedback can the teacher require of the students in order to know whether or not the material that is presented has been comprehended? It is in answer to these questions that one encounters variations within this general delayed oral production framework. James Asher, in his "Total Physical Response," stipulates that at the beginning stages of learning, students should act out commands given by the teacher in the target language. The students mother tongue is avoided (in this respect, these methods can be considered part of the long-popular "Direct Method"), and the students are silent, responding to the teacher by action rather than by speech. Initial commands are quite simple (e.g., "Stand up! Sit down!" with the teacher rising and sitting to demonstrate), but there is an attempt to progress fairly rapidly to more complex activities such as taking a certain book from Student A and carrying it over to Student B in exchange for a certain pencil which is returned to Student A. The teacher can immediately see if the instructions in the target language are comprehended, and there is the belief that learning by doing (enactive learning) is a highly effective means of acquiring new vocabulary and structures. Indeed, Asher and Gary and Gary cite several experiments which reputedly substantiate the success of this form of the delayed oral production approach.

Another classroom procedure is suggested by Postovsky, who originally developed his method while teaching Russian to members of the U. S. armed forces. He spent a few hours the first few days instructing his beginning students in the form of the Cyrillic alphabet which is used for modern Russian orthography, so that they could attempt to write down what they heard and what they wanted to "say" to the teacher and to their classmates. The writing system thus became the vehicle for any classroom responses, so, rather than respond in actions, like the Asher method, the students wrote their comments in Russian. Note that this particular procedure violates the rest of the AL dictum, "speaking before reading, reading before writing." Postovsky, like Asher and other methodologists subscribing to the importance of oral production delay, believed that the students would develop an excellent foundation in Russian by hearing it spoken only by their teacher (who was a native speaker) and would not be confused by their own attempts to pronounce the language. Unlike the "Total Physical Response" designed by Asher, the Postovsky method provided a quiet classroom atmosphere where students were getting a chance to produce Russian words, phrases, and sentences only in written form, not in speech.

Of course, both these methods gradually introduce the student to the spoken form of the target language, the amount of delay varying with the method, the student population, and the goals of the program. Postovsky's method encourages the greatest delay. In his intensive Russian program at the Defense Language Institute reported on in his 1974 paper, his students did not begin speaking Russian in class till after four weeks of daily, full-time exposure! As far as I can surmise, after this important comprehension foundation has been laid and speaking skills are introduced, these methods become indistinguishable from any other method which follows the AL approach. This is an important observation with which to conclude this short discussion of these two methods: that language teaching methods usually differ most at the beginning stages and rapidly become more similar as students progress to more advanced levels of study.

Innovative AL Methods

Within this same AL tradition one can find another group of new methods which are more difficult to characterize than the first group I have discussed. Although these methods concentrate on oral-aural skills and on sequencing of structures in an increasing order of difficulty, they do not insist on an initial period of silent comprehension. They differ from the third type of methodology to be discussed, the interpersonal methods, in that they place linguistics and communicative criteria above interpersonal factors in the design of the syllabus. Two methods that seem representative of what I am calling "Innovative AL Methods" are the Rassias method and the Thomas method. Although both men have been developing their methods for many years, their approaches to language teaching have only recently gained popular support and publicity. Both men originally developed their methods to teach French to Americans but have now expanded their interests to the teaching of other languages and, in some cases, to teaching other subjects beside language as well. What I find interesting about their methods is that, superficially, the procedures followed in the classroom make them appear to be radically different from each other, and from most other methods currently employed; but if one looks carefully at the priorities and the goals of these two methods, they appear to be, in essence, innovations of a traditional AL approach.

The Rassias method, first designed for teaching American university students at Dartmouth College, is characterized by active and intensive interaction between the students and the teacher. The teacher is encouraged to be a whirlwind of activity--in one moment, he will leap across the room to bestow a congratulatory kiss on a student as a reward for a favorable response, but in another instance, he will hurtle back to the other side to throttle another student in a mock stranglehold to punish that pupil for a mistake. All of these gyrations are supposedly planned and orchestrated to give the class a constant stream of reinforcement, either positive or negative, to shape their learning of the target language. When you look beyond these classroom activities to the underlying philosophy of how a language should be learned and taught, all the major tenets of audio-lingualism are immediately apparent: there is the emphasis on spoken, as opposed to written, communication; on active, rapid drilling of students; on the sequencing of materials from easy to difficult; and on the importance of classical conditioning in the shaping of students' responses. According to published reports in the media, the Rassias method is much more popular and effective than traditional varieties of audiolingualism, because of the infectious and dynamic enthusiasm of the teacher (Time 1976; Transition 1981).

The Thomas method, developed in the Los Angeles area over the past thirty years by Michel Thomas, has not had as much publicity as the Rassias method, but I cite it here because it is superficially very diffent from Rassias's approach even though I would also classify it as an innovative AL method. Thomas has designed an elaborate program that is frequently advertised as one that can be used to teach anyone the entire structure of the language in approximately a fortnight. Since the Thomas method is now applied to the instruction of about half a dozen different languages (including English), his claims about the effectiveness of his method are universal--it can work successfully for anyone on any language within a two-week period of concentrated study. Essentially, the program consists of about a week of intensive oral-aural drilling, memory work, and dialogue practice, followed by a week of concentration on reading skills interspersed with teacher-guided discussions of the readings and of topics of general interest. One aspect of this method that is identical to Lozanov's suggestopedia is that all language study is done in class; there is no homework of any kind. The entire program is available on tape, and if one uses the taped series (as most of Thomas's students appear to do), the fact that one can spend up to eight or ten hours per day for seven days in a row listening to casette tapes is enough to distinguish this method from all others known. Like the Rassias method, when one looks beyond the hours of pretaped lessons or the claims of complete mastery within a fortnight, one sees, in essence, a traditional AL approach: oral skills preceding written ones, careful sequencing of grammatical structures, a controlled program of drills, explanations, dialogues, and oral practice, and a generous amount of teacher encouragement.

I do not mean to criticize either the Rassias or the Thomas method by claiming that they are, at heart, renovated forms of the older AL tradition, but I do want to claim that classroom procedures that appear to be quite radical can often be used within the framework of a traditional method. If these two methods are indeed successful, it is because they are capable of motivating students through the use of new techniques in a way that straightforward attempts to teach the AL method have often failed to do.

Interpersonal Methods

It is the subject of student motivation that leads us to the third methodological category under review, the Interpersonal Methods. Stevick, in his well-written and sympathetic analysis of new approaches to foreign language pedagogy, A Way and Ways (1980), uses the term "humanistic" to describe methods like Community Language Learning (CLL) or the Silent Way, but I prefer to call them "interpersonal" rather than "humanistic." The latter label connotes a slightly superior attitude, as if previous attempts were somehow "inhuman." Also, I think it is the concentration on and the fascination with interpersonal factors between students and teachers that set these methods apart, not their preoccupation with learners as human beings. After all, even the most calculating practitioner of the behavioristic AL method is keenly concerned with the problems of human learning and is, in this sense, just as humanistic as any other professional. The essential characteristic that identifies these methods, then, is their attention to interpersonal relationships. In brief, the goal of a foreign language program is to give the language learner a sense of security, independence, and growth, and this goal takes precedence over grammatical considerations and sequencing of linguistic skills.

CLL was developed by the late Father Charles Curran, founder of the Counseling-Learning approach to psychology. It has grown into an active organization that runs workshops and seminars throughout the year and publishes its own materials and monographs.[1] As the words "counseling" and "community" imply, this method is essentially interested in interpersonal factors--in reducing student anxiety, in building a sense of social cohesion in the class, and in helping learners to progress to a stage where they are completely independent of their "counselor's" (teacher's) guidance. As in the other Interpersonal Methods, linguistic structures, sequencing of skills, and classroom drills and exercises are relegated to secondary importance. What makes the CLL approach unique is that students take the initiative in selecting the materials, goals, and the curricular structure for the course. In this sense, CLL is much more student-centered than any other methodology with which I am acquainted.

Like Curran, Caleb Gattegno, founder of the Silent Way, has spent many years developing his methodology and has established his own institute to promote his approach to foreign language teaching--especially ESL.[2] The distinguishing mark of the Silent Way is the strong emphasis placed on inductive learning. This is accomplished primarily through silence on the part of the teacher. Like CLL, this method stresses the importance of the interpersonal relationship between the student and teacher, but rather than centering on what the student does or wants to do, the focus is on the teacher and how the teacher can create situations in which the student can induce useful generalizations about the target language. In the field of ESL in North America, both CLL and the Silent Way have received much

---

[1] CLL has been meticulously described by Stevick (1980), and specific information about the psychological underpinnings of the CLL method itself, especially as it is applied to ESL, can be obtained from the Counseling-Learning Institutes, P.O. Box 383, East Dubuque, IL 61025.

[2] Information about the Silent Way and ESL materials that are available commercially can be obtained from Educational Solutions, Inc., 80 Fifth Avenue, New York, NY 10011.

publicity, and the latter has also been described in detail by Stevick in his recent book; but I think that, of the two, the Silent Way has engendered the most controversy as a method of language teaching, since the technique of having the teacher remain relatively quiet is a direct violation of the major tenet of most modern methodologies, i.e., that the teacher should provide the student with as much aural intake as is reasonably possible.

Concluding Practical Criticisms

The advantages and disadvantages of these six new methods, as well as any method we may choose to employ as classroom teachers, are largely determined by the goals we, or our school, have set for our students. Clearly, there is no one method, no single package of techniques and procedures, which can be used effectively in all situations. Just as obvious however, is the impracticality of mixing a little bit of each method together into one pot, as if we were preparing a soup from all the leftovers available in the kitchen. The compromise between the two extremes is the careful construction of an eclectic method which suits the needs of the students, the teachers, and the society at large. An excellent list of thirteen criteria which typify an effective modern methodology can be found in Haskell's 1978 article on the "eclectic method": "an eclectic methodology (or approach) is one which utilizes the best (most appropriate and/or useful) parts of existing methods" (1978:21). Let me briefly identify what I believe to be the most and the least useful aspects of the methods just described.

The exaggerated emphasis on the importance of listening preceding speaking that is found in the first two methods is unwarranted, both for theoretical and for practical purposes. Much of the recent research in child language acquisition dispels the myth that children spend the first year or two of their lives "passively" listening without producing any meaningful speech. There is a continual progression of speech production from crying, to cooing, to babbling, and up into the holophrastic stage at the end of the first year. It is quite clear that these utterances are all forms of language production. But theoretical criticisms aside, I think most people with classroom experience will realize the universal urge of learners to speak, whatever their age. We do not live in a world where our interlocutors run about silently performing commands or scribling notes to us in reply to our oral questions. I think the traditional AL emphasis on delaying the two writing skills at the early stages of foreign language instruction is well-taken, except perhaps for certain groups of adult learners, but the prolonged delay of oral production is not natural and does not appear to be justifiable as a language teaching procedure. I therefore think that none of the Delayed Oral Production methods can contribute any more to a modern, eclectic methodology than the insights on skill sequencing we have already derived from the traditional versions of the AL approach. An exaggerated stress on a single skill at the introductory stages is impractical, unnatural, and psycholinguistically unjustified. The sole exception might be a program that has a highly circumscribed emphasis on one skill (e.g., training people to monitor radio broadcasts in the target language).

The Innovative AL methods have the advantage of not being overly concerned with skill-sequencing, and at least in this regard, the second two methods are more amenable to being incorporated into an eclectic approach than the first two. Nevertheless, what disturbs me about the second two methodologies is that for each of them, the characteristics that make them unique are the very procedures which I find impractical to recommend as universal recommendations to teachers. No one who has ever seen Rassias in action, either live or on film, can dispute the fact that his theatrical classroom activities are exciting, entertaining, and motivating, but there are two severe practical limitations to his approach: 1) few of us teachers are born with the extroverted dramatic energy of a Rassias, and 2) few foreign language classrooms around the world, for reasons of student age, cultural backgrounds, and pedagogical traditions, are suited for this kind of wisecracking, informal American approach Similarly, I dislike the insistence of the Thomas method on complete mastery of the language within a fortnight and his heavy reliance on long, intensive sessions (usually with a casette recorder). His claims of complete mastery draw a great deal of publicity, but I find no empirical justification for these claims. Just as importantly, the long periods of intensive study are impractical for most of us who teach at schools and universities where foreign language instruction is only one part of a tightly controlled curriculum. Besides, even if we were to instruct our students in intensive two-week blitzkriegs of study, there is no evidence to indicate that 100 hours of intensive language instruction over two weeks is, ipso facto, more effective than 100 hours spread over four months. At best, I believe that the Rassias and Thomas methods can give us some new classroom techniques to consider for adaptation, but not for adoption.

The last pair of methods are probably the best examples of the half-dozen methods under review from which we can draw some practical insights. I do not want to give the impression that CLL and the Silent Way are better than the other four methods. Certainly, we have no proof that this is so, but I do believe that they are more representative of a new and major interest of many ESL teachers in North America today, an interest that can be seen in the number of journal articles and conference papers devoted to this area in the last decade. This is the focus on the interpersonal variables which are important to every classroom, which play such a prominent role in student (and teacher) motivation, and which contribute to the success of any foreign language program. In many instances, it is impractical to adopt the techniques recommended by these two methods. In most EFL or ESL classes I know of, it would not be possible, for example, for the students to make decisions about the materials or the curriculum, as recommended by CLL, nor would it be appropriate for the teacher to engage the class in silent guessing games, as advocated by the Silent Way. But these new methods, taken seriously, do make us think about the effective and motivational forces which are so important in helping us to achieve our pedagogical goals, and I would encourage serious thought regarding these interpersonal factors, along with the traditional linguistic considerations which remain the essential focus of our ESL programs. Although I am not as enthusiastic as Stevick about the importance of interpersonal variables in the language classroom, I recommend his 1980 book as a thought-provoking introduction to some of the new interpersonal methodologies.

Each of the six methods under review has serious limitations, and I, for one, do not believe that new approaches are necessarily good ones. But it is vital to our profession that we continually challenge ourselves, and I hope that this brief review will help teachers to think more seriously and more carefully about what they are trying to achieve with their own language students.

References

Asher, James J. 1979. Motivating children and adults to acquire a second language. SPEAQ Journal 3.3-4.

Gary, Judith O. and Norman Gary. 1980. Comprehension-oriented foreign language instruction--an overview. Linguistic Reporter 23:3.4-5.

Haskell, John F. 1978. An eclectic method? TESOL Newsletter 12:2.19-21.

Kelly, Louis G. 1969. Twenty-five centuries of language teaching. Rowley, Mass.: Newbury House.

Postovsky, Valerian A. 1974. Delay in oral practice in second language learning. Modern Language Journal 58:5-6.229-239.

Scovel, Thomas S. 1979. Review of Suggestology and outlines of suggestopedy, by Georgi Lozanov. TESOL Quarterly 13:2.255-266.

Stevick, Earl W. 1980. Teaching languages: a way and ways. Rowley, Mass.: Newbury House.

Time. 1976. Dynamiting education. August 16, p. 56.

Transition. 1981. Waging war on monolingualism. Winter Issue, pp. 6-8.

Winitz, Harris. 1981. Two considerations in the comprehension of L1 and L2. Conference on Native Language and Foreign Language Acquisition, New York Academy of Sciences, New York, January 15-16.

Language Testing: Where to from Here?*

John W. Oller, Jr.
University of New Mexico

Trends in educational testing in general tend both to respond to and, in some respects, to shape theories and practices in education. Trends in language testing in particular also seem to fit this pattern. Language tests respond to theories and practices in language teaching, and they also help to mold and direct those same theories and practices. The main purpose of this paper is to explore briefly some of the historical trends of language testing and then to look into the present period a bit more deeply and to try to discern what promising directions the theories and practices of the coming years might take. Since the historical picture is relatively well documented in other volumes (see the series of monographs edited by Bernard Spolsky and published by the Center for Applied Linguistics beginning in 1978; also see Oller 1980 and 1983), I will give considerably more space to the present period and what I see as the most promising future directions.

First a brief look at the past.

*This paper has been presented in several versions to a number of audiences. The present rendition was presented at the University of Texas at Arlington on November 3, 1982, and in a somewhat modified form at Brigham Young University at the Deseret Language Conference on April 8, 1983. The shape of the paper presented at BYU was influenced to some extent by the meeting on Performance Testing held at the University of Ottawa in Canada on March 12, 1983. I have been helped in putting the paper together by many colleagues of whom I will mention only a few: H. Douglas Brown, Mark Clarke, Jack Damico, Irwin Feigenbaum, Randal Jones, Steve Krashen, Elizabeth Lantz, Harold Madsen, Adrian Palmer, Pat Richard, and Mari Wesche. Any remaining problems, however, are my own.

Trends in Language Testing

Spolsky (1978) referred to three "periods," or "trends" in language-testing history. He insisted that they could be regarded as trends rather than distinct periods since the earliest period still persisted at the time he was writing some five years ago.

The First Three Periods or Trends

<u>The Prescientific Period</u>. The first period, or trend, Spolsky labeled "prescientific." The pejorative implications of the term were no doubt fully intended. It was a period marked by subjectivity and a rather carefree attitude toward standards. Teachers and administrators alike were at liberty to do just about anything that was considered convenient or traditional under the guise of language testing. For the most part, this meant examinations that frequently required regurgitation of only partly digested, and never fully metabolized, material. Often the test consisted of an essay about some topic concerning which the grader (i.e., teacher or administrator) was an expert and the examinee was a babe in the woods. Memorization and recitation of disjointed facts about literary masterpieces or incomplete and often incorrect analyses of grammar prevailed. Unfortunately, as Spolsky commented in 1978, this trend continues even today in some parts of the world.

<u>The Psychometric-Structuralist Period</u>. Happily, the prescientific trend was largely replaced in many centers of education during the heyday of structural linguistics and the spread of psychometric theory during the 1950s and 1960s (largely by unplanned seepage or osmosis, it would seem). This second period (or trend), dubbed by Spolsky as the "scientific" or "structural-psychometric" trend, saw the rise to power of the multiple-choice test with all of its claims (sometimes greatly exaggerated) to "objectivity." It also saw the entrenchment of the discrete-point theory, as advocated by Robert Lado and by other theorists who enjoyed a certain popularity during this period. In fact, it could well be argued that Lado's insistence on attention to surface forms ("phonemes" and their "allophones," "morphemes" and their "allomorphs," and a largely undeveloped concept of "syntactic structures") was a very natural consequence of the partial understanding of the surface form of language (especially of

"speech" in a rather narrow sense) which was characteristic of linguistic theory both prior to and during the early days of the Chomskyan revolution.

Perhaps the most significant aspect of this second period was its nearly exclusive attention to bits and pieces of language excised from their contexts of use. Almost all of the tests and the vast majority of the language teaching materials of this period were deliberate exercises in nonsense. The point of the teaching and the testing was to drill separate elements of language in a highly analytic manner. As a result, meaning generally was discarded along the way. In fact, the main idea behind the discrete-point item was to escape all the seemingly undesirable (according to the popular theory of the day) benefits of context and meaning. Some theorists, such as Rand Morton, even advocated that students should practice pattern drills the way pianists practice scales and arpeggios--with no intention whatever of communicating (or making music as it were).

The Sociolinguistic-Integrative Period. As might have been expected, of course, the "structural-psychometric period" was challenged in the later 1960s and was largely replaced during the 1970s by what Spolsky termed the "sociolinguistic-integrative" trend. The latter trend stressed the importance of context, and in some ways tended to restore it (ill-defined as it was) to a more respectable place in the hierarchy of applied linguistic concepts. Also, the faddish rise of "integrative" tests such as dictation, cloze procedure, elicited imitation, elicited translation, oral interview techniques, story-retelling, essays, and other long-despised traditional tests tended to offset the much-revered "objective" multiple-choice format.

Furthermore, the clarification during this period of the "instructional value" of tests as a factor to be considered along with "reliability," "validity," and "practicality" also tended to displace some of the confidence in multiple-choice items which were deliberately planned to further confuse the student who was already slightly confused or uncertain about the answer to the question. It was pointed out, for instance, that multiple-choice tests are the only elements of school curricula where the objective is to intentionally lead the student into misconceptions. Moreover, it was also shown that the so-called "objectives" of multiple-choice tests are just as dependent on linguistic intuitions about grammaticality, paraphrase, and meaning as are the so-called "subjective" tests such as oral interview, cloze procedure, elicited imitation, dictation, or essay writing.

The Present Trend: the Pragmatic-Textual Period

Nonetheless, as Spolsky properly notes, the sociolinguistic-integrative trend still continues to a very great extent as do its predecessors. In fact, all three trends survive and remain contemporaries of which I propose to call, following the Spolsky tradition, the "pragmatic-textual trend," The latter trend, as I see it, stems from two theoretical thrusts which can be identified in contemporary language studies. One is the interest in pragmatics--the relationship of texts to the contexts of experience--and the other is what has come to be known as "textlinguistics" or "discourse analysis"--especially popular these days among European linguists.

Due to this fourth trend--or during this fourth period of study, we might say--emphasis has shifted from the surface form of language to its deeper relationships to the contexts of experience. Instead of concern with elements of language cut loose from their moorings in experience, e.g., isolated sounds, or words, or sentences, increasing attention is being focussed on real texts in actual contexts of experience. Beaugrande (1980), for instance, distinguishes between "virtual" texts, e.g., sentences in the abstract, and "actual" texts, e.g., ones that actually occur at specific points in the space-time continuum. While virtual texts may still hold some interest for theoreticians who have little or no interest in pragmatics, those with a practical bent are inclining more and more to the study of texts in the actual settings of real experience.

<u>The Naturalness Constraints</u>. With this shift of interest has come a distinction between merely "integrative" language tests and what may be called "pragmatic" language tests.[1] Any test which mixes modalities (e.g., reading and speaking, or, say, listening, writing, and reading) or components (e.g.,

---

[1] Incidentally, I consider the whole class of what have recently been called "performance" tests, or "performance-based" tests, as essentially indistinguishable from pragmatic texts. For instance, at the meeting on Performance Testing in Ottawa recently (March 11-13, 1983) three types of performance tests were discussed by

phonology, lexicon, and syntax) may be construed as an integrative test, whereas higher theoretical requirements may be placed on pragmatic tests. In fact, I have proposed two pragmatic naturalness constraints on the latter sort of texts. They are, in effect, two sides of the same coin. They may be referred to as the <u>time</u> constraint and the <u>meaning</u> constraint. The first stresses the need for pragmatic language tests to press the examinee into processing under time limits that are characteristic of actual text processing in normal experience. For instance, if a dictation is to qualify as a pragmatic test, the segments to be written down must be presented at a more or less conversational rate (excepting, of course, the pauses between segments which should be long enough to allow examinees to write the material without being extraordinarily fast writers). The second naturalness constraint insists that a pragmatic language test must also require the comprehension of the meaning underlying the text. In other words, if it is possible to do the task without understanding the meaning of what is heard, said, read, written, or just plain contemplated, the task cannot be construed as a pragmatic language test. For instance, a proofreading task in which the reader must ignore the sense of the text in order to, say, find missing structural elements, or to, say, mark out all the <u>f</u>'s, would not qualify.

<u>Pragmatic Language Tests</u>. Putting the two naturalness criteria together results in a definition of a pragmatic language tests as one that requires the pragmatic mapping of meaningful text into meaningful contexts of experience under normal time limits. (We don't expect the grocery store clerk to stand in the aisle all day while we go to the library to find out how to ask, "Where are the potatoes?") As I see it, the principal item on the agenda for the future of linguistics proper is the characterization of the details of this process of pragmatic mapping. Obviously, I will not try to complete this task in the present paper. However, I will undertake to discuss a

---

Randal Jones--(1) direct assessment; (2) samples; and (3) simulation tasks. To the extent that such tests meet the pragmatic naturalness requirements, they are pragmatic tests. To the extent that they fail to do so, I would suppose that they are simply not valid language tests.

number of working hunches which hopefully will provide some clues as to how the nature of this mapping process might be explored. Actually, I am inclined to believe that we get some notion of the significance of this process from the findings of the last decade and a half of language testing research.

One of the unassailable findings of that research is the fact that some rather simple-minded testing techniques work surprisingly well in providing indexes of language proficiency. For instance, oral interviews work rather well, and it does not seem to matter a great deal what material is covered in the interview. Similarly, dictations, much despised during the "structural-psychometric" period, also work rather well just so long as the pragmatic naturalness criteria are respected. Cloze tests of considerable variety work well too. Elicited imitation works. So does essay writing in any number of forms--but especially when the writer is motivated to communicate something significant to some reader(s). Why is this so? Why should techniques, which in a very general way ignore many of the requirements of the discrete-point approaches of the 1950s and 1960s, result in high reliability and validity indices?

Weaknesses in Previous Trends. As I understand it, the "sociolinguistic-integrative" period as defined by Spolsky failed to answer these outstanding questions. Some authors during that period, in fact, tried to deny the clear import of the findings altogether. For instance, Alderson (1979, reprinted in Oller 1983:205-217) contended that cloze tests really were not what they were supposed to be, yet his own research consistently confirmed previous findings.

Similarly, Farhady (1979, also reprinted in Oller 1983:311-322) insisted that discrete-point tests and integrative tests were not really different in their effectiveness. In Farhady's view there should be no difference in the reliability and validity of a phoneme-discrimination task and a text-processing task such as an oral interview. On the contrary, both research and sound, theoretical reasoning controvert this prediction. In fact, the evidence that Farhady appealed to, as I understand it (see my comments on his 1979 paper in Oller 1983:321-322), failed to differentiate between discrete-point and integrative tests. In fact, he himself insisted that in theory the two types of tests were not different. He argued that the distinction between them was founded in a "disjunctive fallacy"--that they really fell along a continuum and were not categorically distinct.

A Categorical Difference between Pragmatic and Discrete-Point Tests. However, if the pragmatic naturalness constraints are taken into account, there exists a subset of integrative tests which are pragmatic in character. This subset cannot by logic include any discrete-point tests. Hence the disjunction of pragmatic tests from discrete-point tests is categorical and the "fallacy" that Farhady concerns himself with evaporates. Incidentally, it may be said that to the extent that the "disjunctive fallacy" obtains between integrative tests of the broader sort (pragmatic tests aside) and discrete-point tests, the whole motivation of discrete-point theory also vanishes. That is to say, if all discrete-point tests are more or less integrative, i.e., not categorically (or qualitatively) distinct from integrative tests, then why all the fuss about cutting elements of language loose from their contexts in the first place? To admit that discrete-point tests cannot be distinguished from integrative tests is to admit that there are no truly discrete-point tests, that such tests are impossible in principle.

The Theoretical Problem of the Present Period

Yet there remains a fundamental theoretical problem in foreign language teaching. That problem is to explain why it so often fails. If the theoretical basis for the "structural-psychometric" trend had been a sound one, how is it that language students exposed to a constant bombardment of utterances in the target language do not necessarily acquire that language? The evidence is overwhelming. Students exposed to utterances without meaning do not acquire much of anything.

Acquisition demands something more than manipulation of target language utterances cut loose from contexts of experience. In the same vein, it has been argued during the recent "pragmatic-textual" period that adequate language testing requires more than a long list of "virtual" texts (i.e., traditional discrete-point items) disassociated from meaningful states of affairs, relationships, and events of experience.

Many Unresolved Questions

However, to insist on "actual" texts rather than "virtual" ones in either teaching or testing of languages is to raise a host of difficult and unresolved questions. If language proficiency is more than linguistic competence in the sense of structural linguistics or Chomskyan theory up to and including 1965, then just what other sorts of knowledge and skill must it include? What components does it contain? Is it more or less holistic in character, or is it fragmented such that tests (and teaching) should address many separate components? How does language proficiency in the sense of "ability to process actual texts" differ from "intelligence" (whatever that is)? How does it relate to "verbal" intelligence, or to "nonverbal" intelligence (Oller 1980)? What about "aptitude"? Are special aptitudes for particular text-processing tasks distince from language proficiency in the more general sense? Just how do they relate to it? How does first language proficiency and its connection with the ability to negotiate experience in general relate to the acquisition of nonprimary language proficiency? Is there any general factor of language proficiency? If so, just how pervasive is it?

It seems to me that these outstanding questions amount to a need for a more adequate theoretical conception not only of language teaching and testing but of how human beings make sense of experience and how it is that they are able to process texts about the world of experience. Moreover, I think that we can learn something significant about this process from the failure of most foreign language teaching.

<u>Why Does Most Foreign Language Teaching Fail?</u> A clue may be found in remarks by Otto Jespersen at about the turn of the century. It was not without humor that he criticized the French texts of his day:

> The reader often gets the impression that Frenchmen must be strictly systematical beings who one day speak merely in futures, another day in <u>passé définis</u> and who say the most disconnected things only for the sake of being able to use all the persons in the tense which for the time being happens to be the subject for conversation while they carefully postpone the use of the subjunctive until next year. (1904:17)

He gave some clue as to what was missing when he suggested that:

> we ought to learn a language through sensible communications; there must be (and this as far as possible from the very first day) a certain connection in the thoughts communicated in the new language.... One cannot say anything sensible with mere lists of words. Indeed not even disconnected sentences ought to be used....(1904:11)

The World of Experience Was Missing. More than half a century later, during the 1960s, Jespersen's thesis was finally put into practice in a Spanish program written by my late father and published by Encyclopedia Britannica Films. The author's preface states:

> We believe that language on the useful, everyday level is situational and sequential and that the moment a student can react automatically...to a given situation identified with his own experience, he "knows" the foreign language used in that situation. The proper procedure then is to immerse the student in the world in which this language is used, a world inhabited by people about whom he knows and cares. This sharing of everyday experiences with people of a foreign tongue creates the climate of sympathy necessary and establishes the sine qua non for the teaching of the language, the desire of the students to learn to communicate with the people of that language ...(Oller 1963:ix).

Episodic Organization

From a theoretical perspective what is required is a clearer idea about what communication is and just how it works. In particular, it may be helpful to begin to understand the sort of organization that Jespersen found absent in his French texts. I would term the missing ingredient episodic organization. It is that design aspect which causes us to regard texts as meaningful (whether written, spoken, or merely contemplated). In particular, episodic organization is the connectedness of events, ideas, and intentions, as well as of the elements of discourse which are often linked to them. Some have argued that this "connectedness" is merely an illusion caused by a Western European outlook. However, this objection may be answered effectively by pointing out, as Karl Lashley did back in the 1950s, that the connectedness of experience is as much a function of physical facts and of physiological mechanisms as it is of psychological tendencies.

With all of the foregoing in mind, four working hypotheses about second language acquisition are considered, each in its turn. These hypotheses form the basis of a discursive investigation of episodic organization. Finally, some obsevations about texts to be used or generated in the course of language instruction and language testing are offered.

The Input Hypothesis

In 1980, Steve Krashen stated explicitly an idea that many language teachers and even some theorists had been considering for a long time. He called it "the input hypothesis." Roughly put, it says that <u>the acquisition of a second language depends on access to and utilization of comprehensible input</u>. Krashen's hypothesis makes it clear that more than mere "access" is required. Or as my father put it some years earlier:

> All teachers of foreign language know that simple "exposure" is not enough.... We all know that until a language becomes an integral part of the student's experience, until he can react to and activate automatically language which has been <u>made a part of his experience</u>, he cannot communicate effectively in the language (Oller 1963:ix).

Of course, this "hypothesis" is not really testable in the traditional sense of experimental science. It is rather a working theory--a sensible basis for practice, and, no doubt, many would also agree that it has some theoretical value as well. Another helpful feature of Krashen's formulation is the idea that to be maximally beneficial, the input should be just a little beyond the student's present stage of development.

Input versus Intake

In an interesting way, the input hypothesis, helps us to formulate the theoretical problem of second language acquisition. The input hypothesis differentiates mere "input" from "intake." The latter is input that gets comprehended. This differentiation helps us to formulate a crucial question: <u>How does input become intake</u>? The question can be represented as shown in Figure 1. The problem is to explain how it is that the leap is made from the spoken or written elements of the target language (INPUT) to comprehension (INTAKE).

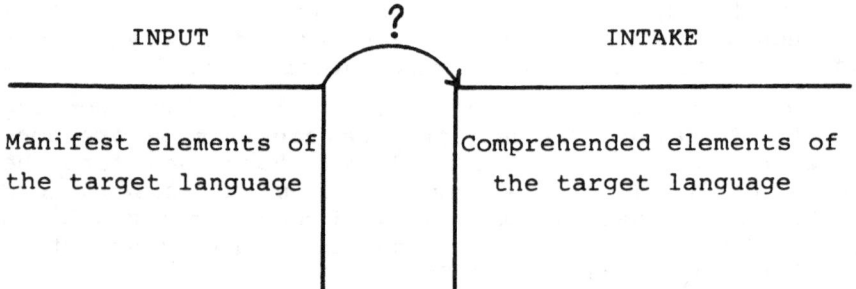

Figure 1. A schematic representation of the language acquisition process as expressed in the input hypothesis.

Pragmatic Mapping

This question, how input becomes intake, can be construed as a special case of the general process of pragmatic mapping. The latter may be defined as the systematic linking of discourse structures to the events of ordinary experience (and vice versa). If we transform Figure 1 into Figure 2, the rough outlines of the process of pragmatic mapping emerge. It is by this mapping process that the event sequences of experience are set in meaningful correspondence with discourse structures.

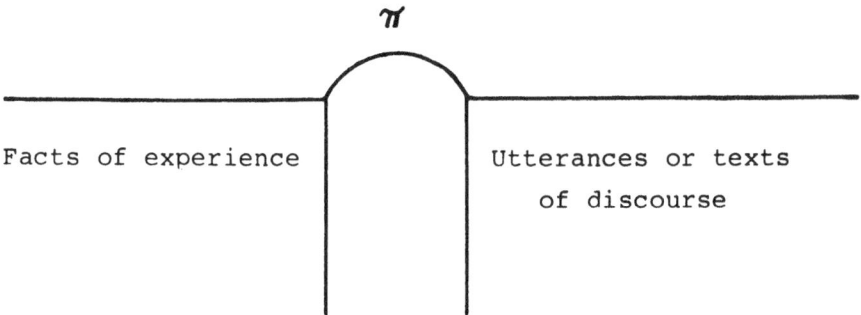

Facts of experience   Utterances or texts
                                of discourse

Figure 2. A schematic representation of the process of <u>pragmatic mapping</u>--the linking of elements of experience with the texts of language.

Input in a second language is merely one of the many types of event structures which constitute ordinary experience. Therefore, the left side of Figure 1 is expanded upon in Figure 2 so as to encompass the broad range of "facts of experience." On the right side of Figure 2 are represented the utterances (or written forms) of discourse, or texts. As with the input hypothesis, the problem is to determine how the inferential leap is made from the facts of experience to the comprehension of discourse. In order to call attention to the inferential pragmatic linkage of the facts of experience with the strings of verbal elements in discourse, the bridge in Figure 2 is labeled with the Greek letter <u>pi</u>.

The process of pragmatic mapping may be construed either at a microcosmic or macrocosmic level. As the microcosmic level the problem is to explain the <u>comprehension</u> of any text, or portion thereof (i.e., to explain the conversion of input to intake, or of experience to text, or vice versa). Also, as will be seen below, the term "text" will be interpreted broadly so as to include realized or inferred sequences of events often referred to as the "contexts of experience." At the macrocosmic level, the problem is to explain the development of language, and still more generally, the advance of knowledge and the maturation of the ability to make sense of experience.

Before going on to discuss the other working ideas closely related to Krashen's input hypothesis, it may be useful to say a bit more explicitly just what the process of pragmatic mapping is. The general problem is one of linking meaningful utterances or their written surrogates with the facts of experience.

<u>Comprehension as Pragmatic Mapping</u>. For instance, consider the foreign visitor at an American airport who read the sign "BUS STOP, NO STANDING" and sat down on the curb. He understood correctly that the "BUS STOP" was a place to catch a bus, but he wrongly interpreted "NO STANDING" to mean that pedestrians were not allowed to stand at the bus stop. The problem was one of pragmatic mapping--correctly linking the elements of the text with the facts of experience. After sitting on the curb for a while it dawned on him that the sign had to apply to drivers passing by in their vehicles. It was the cars that were not supposed to "stand" at the bus stop because they would interfere with the loading and unloading of passengers.

Consider the process. It is necessary to associate the phrase "BUS STOP" with the location where busses, passenger-carrying vehicles, pick up and let off passengers. Similarly, "NO STANDING" must be taken to refer to a class of forbidden actions. The trouble is to determine the subject of the verb "stand" in the underlying deep structure and to relate that structure to a probable referent or class of referents. In this case the intended class of referents consists of persons passing by in automobiles who might be tempted to stop in the way of busses and to load or unload passengers at the bus stop. Therefore, the process of pragmatic mapping is a matter of determining (among other things) referential meaning or deixis. Of course it is more than that because one must also infer antecedent propositional meanings (e.g., the fact that busses stop to pick up and let off passengers) and consequent propositional meanings (e.g., the fact that any car which stopped there would get in the way of the busses). Also, pragmatic mapping involves hooking given propositional structures into whole complexes of relationships between such propositional values.

The foreigner's interpretation of the "BUS STOP, NO STANDING" sign illustrates the sense of the term "pragmatic mapping" as it relates to the immediate problem of comprehension at a particular point in time. It also suggests something of the process of language acquisition in the broader sense of the term. But consider another example which more clearly illustrates the long range effects of pragmatic mapping from the vantage point of language acquisition.

<u>Acquisition as Pragmatic Mapping</u>. Not long ago my wife and I had been out at the malls on a shopping trip to buy an overcoat for me. Son Stephen, age three years and three months, was seated in the back. When there was a lull in the conversation, he said, "I want my [k^{h}o?]." As it so happened the evening was a particularly blustery one and he was already wearing his coat, a fact I pointed out. Naturally, I had "coat" on the brain, having just bought one.

Exasperated he said, "No! I want my [k^{h}o?]."

His mother understood on the second try and handed him the MacDonald's root beer which was between the front seats just beyond his reach as he was buckled in. It had been there all the time while we were in the stores at the mall, ever since our pit stop at the golden arches before the shopping trip began earlier that evening.

Seeing the opportunity for a linguistics lesson and seizing it, I said, "Oh! Son, what you mean is you want your [k^{h}ok^{hhh}]!" I prominently aspirated the final "k."

Stephen repeated, "Yeah Daggy, [k^{h}ok^{hhh}]!" I suppose he is on his way to becoming what Krashen calls a "super-monitor." At any rate, he sharpened up his phonological contrast between final "k" and "t" on the spot. A couple of days later he observed, "I call you 'Daggy', but your real name is 'Daddy', hunh." The "hunh", of course, was uttered with a falling intonation.

What I am getting at is that even the subtlest elements of linguistic surface form get sorted out largely as result of pragmatic mapping--the pressures that arise in linking up the elements of linguistic structure with the facts of experience. These last examples are intended to show that the process of pragmatic mapping extends across time and can be construed as language acquisition itself, or more broadly as the acquisition of knowledge in general.

An Allegory of Pragmatic Mapping as Epistemology

The formula for pragmatic mapping may be construed as a general explanation of epistemology--the acquisition and utilization of knowledge, or making sense of experience. In a rough-and-ready manner, all of this may be pictured allegorically.

Imagine a journey taken by the proverbial homunculus (traditionally supposed to be a minuscule adult male--in the sexist manner of academic tradition) who operates the controls of the information processing center inside the head of the ideal speaker-hearer. For convenience's sake, we will call this character, Pilgrim Elf. Some claim that he normally resides in Cambridge, Massachusetts, but others insist that he stoops to inhabit even the less exalted brains located west of the Mississippi.

In any case, let us suppose that Pilgrim begins his search for meaning with his feet planted firmly on the solid soil of experiential facts. However, as he plods along beyond where, as Kipling might have said, "the roads run out and stop," Pilgrim comes to a vast chasm. There he reads various signs which have been left by previous explorers to help guide him across to the uncharted frontiers of human discourse at the far side of the canyon. The signs warn of great peril. One of them, whose faint inscription seems to bear the signatures of Pierce, James and Dewey, says that travelers who attempt to cross Intelligence Gap without using the Pragmatic Bridge have invariably come to harm. In fact, according to the sign, now weathered with age, some travelers have already crashed to their death on the rocks of experience, while others have been swept away by the River of Reason that flows deep (no one knows who deep) through Intelligence Canyon.

This same sign has an arrow carved in it which points Pilgrim in the direction of the Pragmatic Bridge. The latter arches above the river. Pilgrim notices that its wooden understructure, roughly in the shape of numerous branching trees, is anchored in solid concrete pilings that he supposes must reach to the very Bedrock of Innate Ideas which is believed, by many, to undergird the whole landscape. Venturing out onto Pragmatic Bridge, Pilgrim pauses momentarily to look down at the River of Reason which rages on its course far below. For a dizzy moment, he wonders if it might not have been at this very spot where a research team from MIT tried to float across the river on a raft of logs cut from syntactic trees. According to the newspapers, Pilgrim recalls, due to the manner in which the logs had been cut, they had petrified, and, of course, the raft sank and the researchers were all drowned.

For a while, rapt in awe, Pilgrim just stands there leaning against the rail, contemplating the fact that his right hemisphere is oriented analogically (as it were) toward the holistic facts of experience on the near side of the canyon, whereas his left side is oriented (more or less digitally) toward the highly temporalized texts of discourse at the far side. It occurs to him that the bridge on which he stands is not unlike the <u>corpus callosum</u> of the human brain through which so much information is communicated between the two hemispheres. But, the analogy is an imperfect one, and he soon forgets it and crosses over to the discourse side of the canyon.

Later, as we might have expected, he finds it necessary to make many trips back and forth across the bridge. Even later still, he applies for an MIT research grant, in order to purchase a Helicopter of Abstraction with the aid of which he eventually discovers that the Pragmatic Bridge only appeared to be stationary, that in fact it was interacting dynamically with the two sides of Intelligence Canyon. Further, he concludes that the River of Reason, to his amazement, was only apparently moving. Actually, he surmises, it was the entire landscape that was moving. He later comes to believe (whether rightly or wrongly who can say?) that it is the River of Reason which is actually secure and unmovable.

At this point, we leave Pilgrim as, in any case, he too begins to contemplate the quandaries of the several hypotheses which form the basis for the rest of this paper.

The Three Other Hypotheses

The characterization of the pragmatic mapping process leads to the formulation of three additional hypotheses. They have roughly the same character as the input hypothesis and they serve chiefly to expand upon it and on the process of pragmatic mapping. They, too, are really working hunches, but, like the input hypothesis, they may at least subjectively be tested on the basis of readily available empirical evidence.

Before going into each of them in detail, it may be useful here to preview all three. <u>The textuality hy-</u>

pothesis suggests that the events of experience have a textual character--that they are temporally organized and arranged in sequence. The expectancy hypothesis calls attention to the cognitive momentum that rises and falls during the production or comprehension of discourse, and the episode hypothesis suggests that text (in the sense of any stretch of discourse) will be easier to produce, to understand, to recall, and in general to profit from, if it is episodically organized.

The Textuality Hypothesis

Whereas the diagram of Figure 2 might suggest that the facts of experience are static and solid, by the textuality hypothesis I mean to suggest that the elements of experience themselves are dynamically interrelated and must of necessity be represented in a temporalized logic (sequentialized) in order for us to make sense of them. Further, this hypothesis claims that the highly temporalized event-structures of experience are propositionally complex. Simply put, the textuality hypothesis says that the event-structures of experience are textual in nature. This idea seems to underlie the following remarks by Karl Lashley from his well-known paper on "The Problem of Serial Order in Behavior":

> ...the organization of language seems to me to be characteristic of almost all other cerebral activity. There is a series of hierarchies of organization; the order of vocal movements in pronouncing the word, the order of words in the sentence, the order of sentences in the paragraph, the rational order of paragraphs in a discourse. Not only speech, but all skilled acts seem to involve the same problems of serial ordering, even down to the temporal coordinations of muscular contractions in such a movement as reaching and grasping (italics mine: 1951:187).

Of course, what Lashley is talking about has nothing to do with "Western civilization." He is talking about brain functions--especially the analytic temporalizing functions that seem to be the specialty of the left hemisphere. These functions, probably, are relatively unaffected by differences in the details of culturally determined experience.[2] In other words, the textuality

---

[2] However, there is some evidence that the distribution of brain functions may be determined in part by certain cultural variables in experience (see Sibatani, 1980).

hypothesis argues that event-structures are propositional in nature quite independently of any cultural overlay that may, over the course of development, result in adjustments in their interpretation.

Lashley, however, was focussing his attention explicitly on motoric behavior. The textuality hypothesis is broader in scope. There is an important sense in which all event-structures are temporalized--even when viewed from the vantage point of an independent observer rather than a participant actor. Consider the following example which was originally offered in a slightly different form by someone who was seeking to refute the textuality hypothesis. Suppose that we are observing a worker at an American Embassy somewhere in the Middle East. We note that the crowd outside the Embassy is growing increasingly unruly. Suddenly a brick comes crashing through a window above the worker. He sees it coming and ducks his head just in time. The brick crashes harmlessly to the floor near where he is sitting.

To illustrate the textuality hypothesis it will help if we take a closer look at the event sequence. The important thing to see is that the event sequence itself has a kind of grammatical (propositional) as well as a presuppositional and implicational structure to it.

Why did the brick come crashing through the window? For one thing, it had sufficient momentum to break the glass. But before that could happen, it had to acquire the momentum somehow. We infer that it was thrown by someone. Now notice the sequence of events that is crucial to an appropriate interpretation of the episode. Some unknown person, an agent, throws the brick. That is, the agent acts upon an instrument (the brick) which results in a whole new state of affairs which can be characterized in a proposition or indeed in a whole series of them. The brick hurtles toward the window. After a brief lapse of time, the window becomes a grammatical direct object, whose structure is radically altered by the impact of the brick. The momentum of the brick can be construed as a predication associated with it by the act of the thrower. In order to understand and react to the situation appropriately, it is first necessary to appreciate the fact that the trajectory of the brick would pass through the space now occupied by the head of the worker, if the worker did not negate that propositional possibility by ducking his head. Otherwise, we infer correctly, undesirable consequences would result. To understand this is to take account of a good deal of knowledge about bricks and heads. Setting aside the motoric response of the person who ducks, even for an independent observer to understand this action requires an appropriate interpretation of the textual elements of the event sequence. All of this confirms the textuality of ordinary experience.

The Expectancy Hypothesis

Another hypothesis which relates in fact to both sides of the schematic given in Figure 2 is the expectancy hypothesis. What I propose in this hypothesis is that <u>the activation of correct expectancies will enhance the processing of textual structures</u>. This hypothesis logically applies both to event structures in experience and to the sequences of verbal elements that constitute discourse.

The importance of the effects of expectancies is perhaps best illustrated through errors, or through texts that deviate from the expected form and thus cause us to do a mental doubletake at one or many points while processing them. For example, consider the sentence, "The pen was lost by the pier." The structure is such that we expect an agent (e.g., "by the newswoman") instead of a location "by the pier". What we seem to do in such a case, is like putting on our mental brakes, cramming the gear lever into reverse, and driving by again hoping not to miss the turn. (Expectancies of this sort can conveniently be represented in the sort of grammatical system characterized by Woods 1970; 1978, as an augmented transition network. For a variety of similar examples, see Beaugrande 1980:47-48.)

Expectancies of the most complicated sort enter into even mundane motoric routines. One of my favorite examples came from a certain professor I knew in graduate school. It seems he had just purchased a new cigarette lighter and was driving down the highway at the speed limit. It was a warm summer day and he had the window down. Absently he lit up, shook out the flame, and tossed the lighter out the window. He had developed an expectancy for using matches to light up and continued on automatic pilot to behave as if he had just lit his cigarette with a match instead of a brand new lighter. His error is one of anticipatory mind-set. A sort of cognitive momentum that is set up by a false assumption. Although this example illustrates a problem in the event-structure side of Figure 2, it is not unlike common lexical confusions that occur on the verbal side of intelligence.

For an example of the latter sort, consider the tragically prophetic error of Sadat some years ago. He was asked what he would do if the peace talks with Israel did not bear fruit. He answered that he would turn in his "assassination." He corrected himself immediately and said "resignation," but the fearful motivation for his slip of the tongue had already revealed an anticipatory mind-set--which as it turned out was not unwarranted. Of such errors was Freudian psychology made.

Interestingly, slips of the mind and tongue may also be accompanied by slips of the whole body at times. For instance, I remember an incident where a certain lawyer was preparing to take leave of a tired group of conferees. The long discussions of the day had concluded and people were beginning to look forward to a more pleasant evening. It was the sort of occasion where people are brightening up and congratulating one another on their congeniality. At just such a moment, the lawyer said he would meet the rest of us in the lobby shortly. Then, he turned briskly and ran into the door jamb. Speaking to the wall he said, "Oh, excuse me," and at the same moment gave it a couple of pats as if to say "I hope you're not injured." Then, casting a glance over his shoulder in our direction, he hurried into the corridor and out of sight.

The lawyer's speech act shows that he had formed certain expectancies based on the crowded surroundings and his previous successes at getting through doorways. He apparently was more prepared to run into a person than a door jamb. His error reveals the synchronization required in order for understanding, intention, and action to be properly coordinated.

One final example will serve to illustrate that this coordination involves a delicate synchronization at more than one level of meaning and intention. Not long ago, I was checking out at a grocery store. It was late in the day, and the store was crowded and noisy. The clerk said something to me as I was picking up the bag of groceries to leave. I did not understand and asked for a repetition. She repeated herself. I still missed it, and asked for another shot. She obliged, a bit louder. I still could not quite make out what she had said. On the fourth try, her words were loud enough and mean enough to have stopped the front line of the Pittsburgh Steelers. She shouted, "I said 'T-H-A-N-K Y-O-U!!!" You might have thought that E. F. Hutton had begun to speak. Every head in the store turned.

On what Watzlawick, Beavin, and Jackson (1967) term the "content level", she was apparently intending to say that she was glad I stopped by and that she hoped I would come again. However, due to the difficulty of putting this message (perhaps an insincere one) through the channel, on what Watzlawick et al. term the "relationship level," she ended up saying something like "You idiot, if I never see you again, it'll be too soon."

What this example shows is that plans to communicate must be coordinated in terms of content and relationship information, and also that, as John Dewey observed long ago, the things that one says may often surprise oneself as much as anyone else. My third hypothesis provides a basis for linking the textuality and expectancy hypotheses to each other and to Krashen's input hypothesis.

The Episode Hypothesis

The episode hypothesis says that text (i.e., discourse in any form) will be easier to produce, understand, and recall to the extent that it is motivated and structured episodically. A corollary to this hypothesis is that the acquisition of a second language will be facilitated to the extent that the texts used in the instructional process are episodically organized. There are two aspects to "episodic organization"--motivation (or effect) and logical structure. Generally, it may be said that selling authors respect both of these (Braine 1974, Peck 1980, and Swain 1980).

Before we go on to consider the motivation and structure of episodically organized texts, it is necessary to show that the episode hypothesis and its corollary relate to second language teaching. It seems to me that these ideas lead to the supposition that perhaps second language teaching would be more successful if it incorporated principles of good story writing along with the benefits of sound linguistic analysis. This supposition underlies all of the preceding discussion. We will return to it shortly to consider some of the ways in which it may help to bolster practical approaches to language teaching, but not it is time to illustrate more explicitly what episodic organization is.

As with the expectancy hypothesis, episodic organization may be clarified by examining cases where it is violated. There are two principal ways in which episodic organization can be made light of. The first common violation is to generate unmotivated (or poorly motivated) text. The result, as Peck observes, is "dull, dull, dull," and most writers who do it, unless they happen to write for ESL or FL publishers, generally remain unpublished. Speakers who do it are rarely invited back for a second engagement. The person who persists in it is regarded as a bore.

The second common violation is to generate illogical (or jerky) text. This may prove interesting in the short term (provided it is motivated), but usually it loses its audience much as a devilish bronc unseats many a would-be rider. The result of the two types of violation together is almost always fatal to the text. The first violation usually quenches the spirit of any potential interpreter, and the second skins the shins and twists the nose of the unfortunate Pilgrim until he gives up and goes home.

Textual Logic. Let us take the problem of textual logic first. My favorite example of an apparent narrative which jerks and twists and turns with tortured logic comes from the 19th century humorist, Samuel Foote. It is a useful piece of text because though it violates the principle of episodic structure, it has a surprising episodic motivation, which we will come to in a moment. But first let us take a look at the text:

> So she went into the garden to cut a cabbage leaf to make an apple pie: and at the same time a great she-bear coming up the street pops its head in the shop. "What! No soap!" So he died, and she very imprudently married the barber: and there were present the Picninnies, the Joblillies, and the Garcelies, and the great Panjandrum himself, with the little round button at the top, and they all fell to playing the game of catch-as-catch-can, till the gunpowder ran out the heels of their boots (S. Foote, ca. 1854, as cited by Cooke 1902:221f).

My father used to quote this passage as part of a general sales pitch on the importance of "meaningful sequence" (alias "episodic structure") in materials to be used for teaching a foreign language. His point was that the logic of the text is not terribly unlike that found in many exercises written for the consumption of foreign language students. Except for its vague resemblance to narrative and its syntactic heterogeneity, Foote's prose would well pass for many an ESL or FL pattern drill from a now, we may be grateful, fading era.

The trouble with Foote's prose is not so much its violation of what might be construed as a purely Western style of episodic organization of discourse; rather, it is a problem of how to make an apple pie, and of the habits and haunts of she-bears. It is a matter of shaving soap, mortality, and barber shops, of weddings and the kind of folk who celebrate them. Of gunpowder and boot heels.

However, if we look back at the time and place where Foote's text was created, we discover that in fact his prose was not "unmotivated" in the sense in which we used this term above. That is, Foote himself had a pragmatic purpose in mind. His text made a point. It was a practical experiment proving one aspect of the episode hypothesis. To see this, we must look back at the context of his creation.

It seems that Foote had been attending a series of lectures where a certain Professor Macklin was holding forth on the art of oratory. On the evening in question, Macklin boasted that using the techniques of memorization which he had ardently recommended throughout, and which he himself had mastered, he could repeat by rote any passage of prose up to a hundred words in length after having read it aloud only once. Foote casually wrote the text about the she-bear and the barber shop on the back of a scrap of paper, handed it to Macklin, and challenged him to read it once and repeat it from memory.

To the great delight of Mr. Foote, Macklin read the text, but, alas, after only one pass through it, was unable to repeat it from memory. With a single stroke of humorous fantasy, Foote reduced Macklin's boast about his memory to a scrambled mess of apple pie and cabbage leaves. The trouble was that Macklin <u>could</u> memorize up to a hundred words in a single <u>pass</u>, provided the words fell into the sort of meaningful sequence characteristic of the logic of ordinary prose.

In retrospect, we look back and say that Foote's prose was pragmatically <u>motivated</u> by Macklin's boast, but the text itself <u>violated</u> many of the constraints that govern ordinary narrative. His prose lacked the internal episodic structure of ordinary discourse.

<u>Motivation</u>. Of course, there are lots of examples of texts that are poorly motivated and/or poorly structured. In fact, lack of motivation especially may be singled out as one of the most common faults in texts that are written for the consumption of second language learners. For instance, consider the following conver-

sation that supposedly took place on an airplane while Mr. and Mrs. Miller were en route to Hong Kong. They had run into Miss Yamada again, a stewardess they had met on an earlier flight. Miss Yamada had begun to show them pictures of family and friends, and then the following dialog is supposed to have ensued:

> Miss Yamada: This is my best friend. Her name is Fumiko.
>
> Mrs. Miller: She's very pretty. Is she older or younger than you?
>
> Miss Yamada: She's one year younger.
>
> Mrs. Miller: Aren't you thinner than she is?
>
> Miss Yamada: Yes, I am. Fumiko loves to eat.
>
> Mr. Miller: So do I. I hope it will be time for lunch soon.

(National Council of Teachers of English 1973:73).

This text is odd because it lacks motivation. For instance, we might ask why the dialog takes place. Does it have anything to do with getting to Hong Kong? Actually, in a tangential way it does, but it does not seem to contribute toward that end in any significant way. (It is not the sort of thing that one would be apt to write home about.) More particularly, we might ask why Mrs. Miller is curious about the relative ages of the stewardess and her friend. Or, why Miss Yamada happens to take out the picture album in the first place. However, once the pictures are out, why is Mrs. Miller so curious about the relative sizes of Fumiko and Miss Yamada? Is the picture so bad or the stewardess's uniform so ill-fitting that the question is not superfluous--not to mention impertinent?

It is not so much that the text lacks structure. On the contrary, Mrs. Miller seems to have an abiding concern for "structure"--especially comparatives. (She is probably an ESL teacher of the old school.) There is even a kind of temporal development in the conversation as, for instance, the mention of eating causes Mr. Miller to remark upon the fact that it is lunch time. What is missing is a motivation for Miss Yamada to take out the pictures in the first place, or for Mrs. Miller to ask about relative ages and weights, or alternatively to quiz Miss Yamada on her ability to use English comparatives. Also, there is the general question as to why this conversation is reported in the course of a trip to Hong Kong.

What exactly is missing from the Miller text, and

from many similar ones in ESL or FL texts? Or, putting the question differently, how is it that the episode does not seem to make any essential contribution to the Millers' experience, or even to their trip to Hong Kong? Wouldn't it make more sense to delete the dialog and just report, "The Millers went to Hong Kong by plane"? Apparently, the hidden agenda is to give the ESL students practice in the use of comparatives. This is probably the true motivation not only for the dialog, but for the chance meeting on the plane, and perhaps even the trip to Hong Kong in the first place. However, any such motive is simply insufficient if we take the pragmatic basis of trips to Hong Kong and the like seriously. Yes, giving practice in the use of comparative structure is a kind of pragmatic motive (to an ESL textbook writer), but it is to esoteric as a motive to contribute to an interesting story. The interpreter (listener-reader-hearer-learner) remains unmotivated. The outcome, in the words of Peck, is "dull, dull, dull."

What is missing?

Conflict. A little more than seven decades ago, John Dewey (1910) noted that reflective thinking is always occasioned by trouble. A difficulty arises in experience and provides the incentive for reflection. Without any trouble there just isn't anything much worth bothering your head about. Not only is there nothing to write home about, there isn't even anything to converse about. Dialog that contains no implicit conflicts, that wrestles with no troubles or difficulties, is a lot like reflective thinking without any trouble. It is, in short, unmotivated.

Interestingly, Dewey's analysis of thinking presupposes that human behavior is goal-directed. There can be no trouble except in relation to thwarted purposes or desires. The very definition of the term "trouble" implies a cognitive superstructure with goals and plans to achieve them. (For analyses attempting to characterize such structures more explicitly, see Schank and Abelson (1977) and Rumelhart (1975). However, we may note in passing that Rumelhart's story schema does not say anything significant about the beginnings and ends of stories precisely because he does not concern himself with explaining where conflict enters and exits.)

Perhaps the single most common goal-orientation of human beings (something that can be taken for granted in <u>almost</u> all contexts of ordinary life) is the struggle to preserve life against the threat of death. This is a very practical version of the classic conflict of good and evil which appears in most novels in one form or another. Just such a classical structure motivates man's religious activities. The universal problem would seem to be the achievement of enlightenment and immortality.

Even scientific endeavors, in a very general sense, can be construed as attempts to differentiate false propositions from true ones, correct theories from nonsense. Presumably the fact that false ideas and superstitions in the end promote disease, poverty, and injustice is the primary motivation for the pursuit of scientific thinking and research.

Or, putting the whole perspective of episodic organization in a nutshell, we may refer to Robert Newton Peck's observation that "a plot is two dogs and one bone." Conflict in the pursuit of desired ends provides the motive for conversation, for writing home, and for telling stories as well as listening to them. A meaningful episode, one worth generating text about, is one that involves an experiencer pursuing a desirable goal in the face of opposition--the more severe the opposition, the more desired is the goal, and the more motivated will be the telling, comprehending, recalling, and retelling of the story. Or, casting the whole matter in Piagetian terms (see especially, Piaget 1981), it may be argued that conflict is the principal source of the effective fuel that powers the cognitive engine. Dwight Swain (1980) and other teachers of writers have also often commented on the importance of feeling as a reaction to conflict and as a motivation for storytelling.

The episode hypothesis thus asserts that to the degree a text is episodically organized (motivated and structured episodically), it will be easy to produce, understand, recall, and otherwise to benefit from for any practical purpose. To illustrate this, consider the fact that there are answers to many questions in reference to episodically organized texts which elicit only a blank stare when asked in reference to less-organized texts. For instance:

> Why did the she-bear amble up the street?
>
> Who died in the barber shop?
>
> What killed him, the lack of soap or the bear?

> How did the gunpowder end up inside the boots of those at the wedding?
>
> What is the game of catch-as-catch-can?

For these questions there are no determinate answers because the text in question lacks the requisite level of episodic structure (i.e., meaningful sequence).

The same is true, though less dramatically so, of the Miller text:

> Why did Miss Yamada take out her picture album?
>
> Why does Mrs. Miller ask about the relative ages of Fumiko and Miss Yamada?
>
> How does the conversation with Miss Yamada relate to the Millers' trip to Hong Kong?

Compare the absence of any determinate answers for the foregoing questions with the following:

> Why did the Embassy worker duck his head?
>
> What would have happened if he hadn't ducked?
>
> What caused the brick to come crashing through the window?

Or, consider the determinacy of the answers concerning the Foote text if we focus on the broader episodic context which motivated Foote's creation:

> Why did Foote write such an extraordinary text?
>
> Why couldn't Professor Macklin repeat it?
>
> What does Foote's demonstration prove about memory?
>
> Who had the better understanding of memory, Macklin or Foote?

And, obviously, many other questions could be adduced.

However, the point is by now established: <u>to the extent that a given text is episodically motivated and structured, it will give a richer yield of information</u>. Quite simply, it contains a larger quantity of accessible information than a less structured text.

Some Implications

So where does all of this lead us? What can we conclude from the input, textuality, expectancy, and episode hypotheses? It seems to me that several significant implications can be drawn for second language instruction, and for education in a more general sense as well. These can perhaps best be summed up as caveats which, as I indicated above, have their roots in successful story writing techniques. I am thinking here primarily in terms of second language instruction, but no doubt some of the implications which I will try to make explicit seem to have applications to instructional objectives in other areas of school curricula.

First, I think that unmotivated texts should be avoided. We should treat them just as we would polecats with their tails in the air. Since, as we saw above, motivation seems to hinge on meaningful conflict, a text that lacks conflict relevant to the pursuit of a desired goal should not be used. This will <u>help</u> to relieve a lot of classroom boredom.

Second, the story line should be carried primarily by stageable action. This piece of advice comes from the most successful fictionalist of all time, Erle Stanley Gardner, and has been echoed many times by other successful writers. By 1979, Gardner had sold 310 million copies of his novels--mainly the mystery novels featuring Perry Mason and company. According to a 1981 publisher's release (Ballantine Books in New York), Gardner still outsells Agatha Christie, Harold Robbins, Barbara Cartland, and Louis L'Amour combined. Therefore, it seems that the advice he wrote in a letter to an aspiring writer is worthy of our attention:

> Don't say that the villain is a mean man with a wicked wallop. Show him sliding down from his horse in a rage because the animal jerks away from him. Show him swing a terrific fist and crash the horse on the nose. That gives the reader the idea of the wickedness of his wallop. Then when the villain advances toward the hero with doubled fist the reader gets some suspense because he's seen what happened to the horse. But if you tell the reader the villain is bad and has a mean wallop it's history, and the less history you get into a yarn the better (as cited by Fugate and Fugate 1980:79).

Or, in the words of Robert Newton Peck, "Don't tell 'em: show 'em."

If this advice were heeded in the preparation of materials to be used in teaching languages, texts would be easier to dramatize, easier to understand, and much effort presently wasted trying to make sense out of nonsense could be better used.

Third, if the action of the story line is to be stageable, it must respect the logic of experience. (And to a surprising degree this is even true of fantasy.) That is to say, the sort of pattern drill nonsense that goes through every imaginable permutation of a given surface form without respect to meaning should never be used. In other words, we should not ask language students to practice drills like the following:

John is a pilot.

John is not a pilot.

Is John a pilot?

If John were a pilot, he could fly an airplane.

John is not a pilot so John cannot fly.

John is a pilot so John can fly.

If John were not a pilot, he could not fly.

Be a pilot, John, so you can fly.

Fly to the John, pilot.

Ask the pilot where the John is, John.

The John is not a pilot.

The pilot is not a John.

For the non-native speaker there is little possibility of comprehending drills which permute structures without regard for meaning, and even less motivation to do so. In fact, meaningfulness is contrary to the intent of meaningless drills in the first place. However, meaningless drills are not logically necessary. Pattern drills, where they are used, may be anchored in pragmatically motivated text. For instance, in connection with his Spanish program my father wrote:

> Even the structure drills...are either based upon the known facts of the story or are cued by means of cartoons so as to render comprehension automatic.... (Oller 1963:x)

Fourth, from the earliest stages of second language acquisition, it makes sense to present the experience side of the pragmatic mapping first, and then go on to analyze in greater detail the discourse side. In other words, the teacher should first make sure the students know what happens in the story, who is there, where it all takes place, what difference the events make to the characters, and what goals are being sought and thwarted. Then the student will be in a position to begin to work out an understanding of the subtleties of the target language used in that text in much the same manner, presumably, that the first language acquirer develops the usual sort of native-speaker "intuitions."

Fifth, if the text is long it may be broken down into manageably smaller chunks. Understanding a long text is like eating an elephant in this respect: both must be consumed one bite at a time. This principle lays to rest many a complaint that texts in general are "too complicated for learners at stage X" (where "X" may be any point between ground zero and native-speaker competence).

Sixth, it will be possible with episodically organized material to work through each episode in multiple cycles where the depth of understanding and the range of comprehension increase on each pass. On the first pass through a text or segment only the bare outlines may be understood. On the second and subsequent passes, progress is made from the principal facts of who, what, and where, to the meatier details of when, why, and how, and eventually to presuppositions, associations, and implications at whatever depth suits the purpose of the instructor.

In the final analysis, the process of pragmatically linking input in the target language with the facts of experience depends on comprehension, as Krashen, Burt Dulay, and other have argued. This process can be faciliated by capitalizing on the textuality of ordinary experience, respecting its logic, harnessing the cognitive momentum that this logic creates, and in general by employing good story-telling techniques in preparing, packaging, and presenting language teaching materials.

References

Alderson, J. Charles. 1979. The close procedure and proficiency in English as a foreign language. TESOL Quarterly 13.219-228. [Also in Oller, 1983, 205-217.]

Beaugrande, Robert de. 1980. Text, discourse, and process. Norwood, New Jersey: Ablex.

Bobrow, Daniel G. and Allan Collins (eds.). 1975. Representation and understanding. New York: Academic Press.

Braine, John. 1975. Writing a novel. New York: McGraw Hill.

Cooke, William (ed.). 1902. The table-talk and bon-mots of Samuel Foote. London: Myers and Rogers.

Dewey, John. 1910. How we think. Boston: D. C. Heath.

———. 1916. Essays in experimental logic. New York: Dover.

Farhady, Hossein. 1979. The disjunctive fallacy between discrete-point and integrative tests. TESOL Quarterly 13.347-357. [Also in Oller, 1983, 311-322.]

Fugate, Francis L. and Roberta B. Fugate. 1980. Secrets of the world's best-selling writer: The story telling techniques of Erle Stanley Gardner. New York: Morrow.

Jespersen, Otto. 1904. How to teach a foreign language. London: Allen and Unwin.

Krashen, S. D. 1980. The input hypothesis. In James E. Alatis (ed.), Current issues in bilingual education. Washington, D. C.: Georgetown University. [Also in Oller 1983, 357-366.]

Lashley, K. S. 1951. The problem of serial order in behavior. In L. A. Jeffress (ed.), Cerebral mechanisms in behavior. New York: Wiley. [Reprinted in Sol Saporta (ed.), 1961. Psycholinguistics: A book of readings. New York: Holt, Rinehart and Winston. 180-198.]

National Council of Teachers of English. 1973. English for today, Book two: The world we live in, Second edition. New York: McGraw Hill.

Oller, John W. 1963. Teacher's manual: El espanol por el mundo, primer nivel. Chicago: Encyclopedia Britannica Films.

Oller, John W., Jr. 1981. Language as intelligence? Language learning 31.465-492.

———. (ed.) 1983. Issues in language testing research. Rowley, Mass.: Newbury House.

Peck, Robert N. 1980. Secrets of successful fiction. Cincinnati, Ohio: Writers Digest.

Piaget, Jean. 1947. The psychology of intelligence. Tottowa, N. J.: Littlefield Adams.

———. 1971. Genetic epistemology. Tr. E. Duckworth, New York: W. W. Norton.

———. 1981. Affectivity and intelligence. Trs. and Eds. T. A. Brown, C. E. Kaegi, and Mark R. Rosenzweig. Palo Alto, CA: Annual Reviews.

Rumelhart, David E. 1975. Notes on a schema for stories. In Bobrow and Collins, 211-236.

Schank, Roger C. 1975. The structure of episodes in memory. In Bobrow and Collins, 237-272.

———. 1980. Language and memory. Cognitive Science 4.243-284.

——— and Robert Abelson. 1977. Scripts, plans, goals, and understanding. Hillsdale, N. J.: Lawrence Erlbaum.

Sibatani, Atuhiro. 1980. The Japanese brain. Science, December 1980, 24-27.

Spolsky, Bernard. 1978. Introduction: Linguists and language testers. In Bernard Spolsky (ed.), Approaches to language testing. Advances in language testing series: 2. Arlington, Va.: Center for Applied Linguistics.

Swain, Dwight V. 1981. Techniques of the selling writer. Norman, Oklahoma: University of Oklahoma.

Watzlawick, Paul, Janet H. Beavin, and Don D. Jackson. Pragmatics of human communication. New York: W. W. Norton.

Woods, William A. 1970. Transition network grammars for natural language analysis. <u>Communications of the Association for Computing Machinery</u> 13.591-606.

———. 1978. Generalization of ATN grammars. In William Woods and R. Brachman (eds.), <u>Research in natural language understanding</u>. Cambridge: Bolt, Beranek, and Newman (<u>Quarterly Progress</u> Tr 4. 3963).

Applied Linguistics: The Use of Linguistics in ESL

Christina Bratt Paulston
University of Pittsburgh

An exhaustive bibliography on the topic of this paper would fill pages, for linguists have written extensively on the subject. They have also disagreed extensively--from Newmark's "The transformationist's analysis of verb phrase constructions, beginning with Chomsky's simple C(M) (have+en) (be+ing) V formula, brings startling simplicity and clarity to our understanding of the grammatical structure of a number of discontinuous and elliptical verb constructions; transformational grammar seems to offer suggestions neatly and precisely for what a program teaching English verb structure would have to include" (1970:213); to Chomsky's own "Frankly, I am rather sceptical about the significance, for the teaching of languages, of such insights and understanding as have been attained in linguistics or psychology" (1966:43), and "It is the language teacher himself who must validate or refute any specific proposal" (1966:45). Who is right? In a sense, that is what this paper is about.

If by "applied linguistics," we mean the use linguists put their knowledge to in order to get things done in the real world, it is immediately clear that applied linguistics means a lot more than merely language teaching (Corder 1975; Roulet 1975; Spolsky 1978). It is generally recognized that translation is one aspect of applied linguistics, but in this context it is less frequently pointed out that translation existed centuries before linguistics, and, in fact, provided a powerful impetus for the development of the discipline of linguistics in the United States. Missionaries, in groups like the Wycliffe Bible Translators and the Summer Institute of Linguistics, were dedicated to spreading the Word of God by translating the gospels into primarily unwritten languages. They found that they made awkward mistakes. To give but one example: many languages have inclusive we ('all of us guys') and exclusive we ('my friend and I but not you guys'), and if one has never run into them before, the inclusive/exclusive feature of the first person plural pronoun is far from immediately apparent. So it is not surprising that the missionaries inadvertently translated "Our Father" with exclusive we, and subsequently discovered to their horror the Aymara Indians' interpretation of a God for white folk only, which notion was the last on earth they had intended. Accordingly, scholars like Kenneth Pike of the Summer Institute of Linguistics in Phonemics: A Technique for Reducing Languages to Writing (1947), Eugene Nida of the American Bible Society in Morphology: the Descriptive Analysis of Words (1949), and later H. A. Gleason of the Hartford Seminary Foundation in An Introduction to Descriptive Linguistics (1955), were concerned with what came to be known as "discovery procedures," the analysis of unknown and unwritten languages.

One result of the practical bent of anthropologists and missionaries was that it inadvertently developed techniques for language learning through the focus on discovery procedures such as substitution drills. Partially, I suspect, the audio-lingual method, also known, albeit erroneously, as the linguistic method, was a historical accident created in war time by linguists who turned to their established procedures for getting things done. The point I am making here is that there is very much a two-way street between theory and application, between translation/linguistics and language learning, and that problems in the real world do touch and test the development of theory. Linguistics as we know it today would never have existed if people had not tried to do things with language, all the way back to Panini. We clearly have to reject a model like Figure 1 (Roulet 1975:71) as inaccurate and misleading, where the direction of influence is only one way.

There are two ways to answer the question of the significance of linguistics for language teaching. One is to argue from theory to speculative claims in a logico-deductive manner, as Newmark does. The evidence for his "startling simplicity and clarity" claim is his own expert opinion. This is by far the most common approach, and the literature is replete with grand

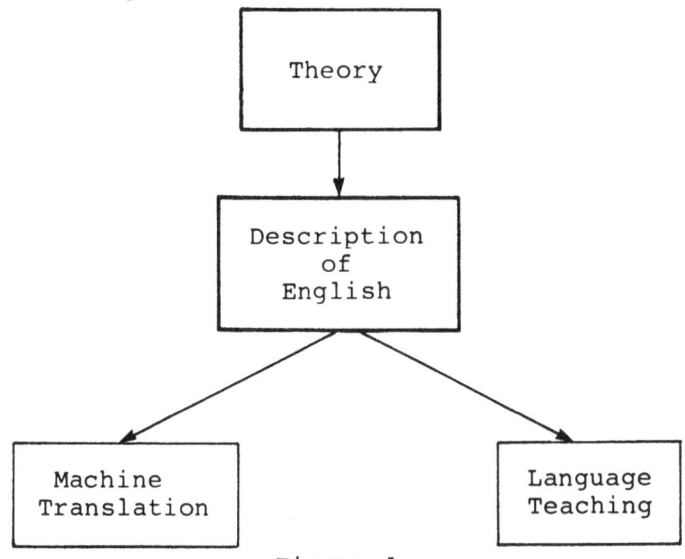

Figure 1

claims of what linguistics can achieve for the language learner. Furthermore, these claims cannot be dismissed on the grounds that there is no evidence to support them, for they are made by men of stature and experience with language teaching, as seen in works like Fries (1954), Lado (1957), Moulton (1961), and Allen and Corder (1975), to pick three classics and one more recent work.

The other way is, of course, to argue from data and to document the use of linguistic insights and knowledge in the classroom. We could ask the teachers of ESL what they find helpful from their training in linguistics and what they actually use in the classroom. Such data will share the weakness of all self-report data and should therefore be augmented by actual classroom observation where the observer especially watches for any evidence of the use of linguistic knowledge. One can examine syllabi and textbooks for similar evidence, as well as consider the claims in recent journal articles with a practical bent, the latter also being a type of self-report data. One might consider examining the content of teacher training courses, but actually I think this would reveal only that the director considered such content important, not whether the teachers in fact would ever use such knowledge.

I have attempted a rather cursory investigation of this kind. Our English Language Institute, modelled after the Michigan ELI, teaches English to some 200 students with some twenty-five instructors (the exact figures vary from term to term). Sixteen instructors (most of them assistants in the Department of Linguistics) returned questionnaire responses in which they were asked to rate the usefulness of their course work for teaching purposes on a scale from 1 to 10. I interviewed seven TA's who were students in a supervision seminar. I observed classes and immediately found an interesting research problem.

In none of the three grammar classes I observed was there any indication that the instructors had any linguistics training beyond a good public school ninth grade class with Warriner et al (1975); nor was there any overt, clear, solid, unmistakable evidence that the teacher was a linguist in the making. I confess that this fact surprised me. One of the instructors was a young man in the throes of his doctoral linguistic comprehensive exams, which is possibly the time in one's life of the most intense consciousness of matters linguistic. In an in-depth interview following my observation of his class, he made the following points: 1) He didn't use technical linguistics terms in the class room (beyond 'indirect/direct object focus in active/passive transformation') for the simple reason that the students would not understand it. (This attitude permeates the instructors' thinking in general.) 2) He found his knowledge of syntax very useful in selecting teaching points, i.e., what to teach and what to ignore about the passive construction as well as setting up and presenting the construction in model sentences on the board and in the explanations. 3) He thought the text book exercises awful and that the best approach to teaching the passive is not through transformations of formal aspects of the active voice.

In essence, what we have here are cognitive and attitudinal influences of linguistics on the instructor which are not observable but nevertheless of extreme importance. It is a situation similar to establishing avoidance behavior in socio-linguistics, a very difficult problem. To compound the difficulty, we have an aspect of Labov's "observer's paradox." The young man had previously been admonished by his regular supervisor to beware of too much teacher-talk, and we cannot exclude the possibility that he monitored carefully any linguistics jargon in my presence. Participant observation is not a sufficient approach to data collection in problem areas which are so cognitively oriented as linguistics and teaching.

A third point should be made. It is surprising after twelve years of classroom observation in the ELI that I should be surprised. I take linguistics for granted and have just never looked for it, so to speak. The lack of its manifest presence, when I was specifically looking, surprised me.[1] This fact suggests a third way for answering our question about the significance of linguistics for language teaching, namely putting the two approaches together and using theory to guide our looking for supporting data, a common enough approach in experimental research. The model I propose using is Roulet's (1975:83) (Figure 2):

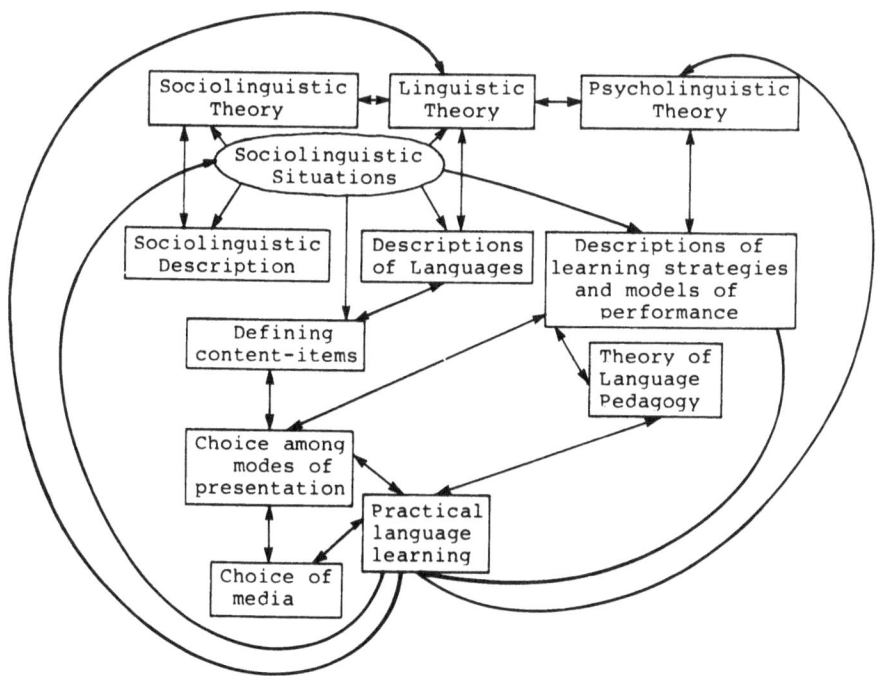

Figure 2

---

[1] Had I gone to a pronunciation class, I would have found lots of evidence of phonetics.

His major point, which others have made before him (e.g., Spolsky 1969), is that various fields besides theoretical linguistics contribute to language teaching and that one needs to understand the processes of their interrelationship as well. I propose to use Roulet's categories as a check list for examining the possible contributions to language teaching we might find from linguistics in this broad sense of the word and then to look for evidence that they occur somewhere in the teaching process.

Sociolinguistic Theory

This topic might usefully be divided into two categories: sociology of language and sociolinguistics. The sociology of language deals with language problems and language treatments at the national level as problems arise within and among ethnic and national groups in contact and competition. Choice of national language and of writing system, language standardization, bilingual education, language maintenance, and shift efforts are all examples of language problems. Naturally, ESL is affected by the choice of teaching Nigerian children to read in English and teaching Chicano children to read in Spanish and in English, but it is more at a level of global understanding of contextual means and constraints than at a direct classroom level of application.

"Sociolinguistics" refers to an approach to description of language which takes into account the social features of a far-from-ideal hearer-speaker and seeks to account for the rules of linguistic variability, be it social, regional, cultural, gender, register, or stylistic variation. (Labov has made the claim that the term "sociolinguistics" is tautological since all linguistics needs to do this.) Sociolinguistics is probably the area which has most influenced language teaching developments within the last ten years, especially through its work with sociolinguistic description on speech acts, pragmatics, discourse analysis, and cross-cultural communication. There is no one sociolinguistic theory, and sociolinguists use notions and concepts from several disciplines, primarily from anthropology, linguistics, and sociology. The work of Hymes, Labov, and Bernstein may serve as representative examples. Hymes' notion of "communicative competence," which draws on key concepts in ethnography, has, more than any other theoretical model, influenced a new direction in language teaching (see below). Labov's work on Black English (1969) helped to legitimize this dialect with formal descriptions of its rule-governed behavior, and to dispel ideas of sloppy, lazy speech. The interest in SESD (Standard English as a Second Dialect), as this special interest group is known in TESOL, and the many resultant publications (Baratz and Shuy 1969; Dillard 1972; Fasold and Shuy 1970; Kochman 1972; Feigenbaum 1970; Mitchell-Kernan 1971; Wolfram 1969; Wolfram and Clarks 1971), peaked in the late sixties and early seventies, and at present it forms a less-viable part of ESL. But the interest is bound to return, because the basic problems are still with us; since the basic groundwork was done in sociolinguistics, I am reasonably certain (I speak as a former SESD chairman) that ESL--or rather TESOL--will continue to be its spiritual and organizational home, an example of applied linguistics at its very best.

The attempts to explain, at a theoretical level, the educational failure of lower-class and minority children have been many and varied: from Jensen's genetic model (1969), through cultural deprivation (Bereiter and Engelmann 1966), to cultural differences (Abrahams and Troike 1972; Burger 1971; Cazden et al. 1972; Saville-Troike 1976; Spolsky 1978; Trueba and Barnett-Migrahi 1979). Much of the linguistic work on Black English was motivated by the linguistic ignorance of the psychologists who wrote about the language of Black children. Another series of theory-building which has marginally found its way into ESL, but has nevertheless greatly influenced the thinking of sociolinguistics, is that of the British sociologist Basil Bernstein (1971; 1972; 1973). He posits the notions of restricted and elaborated code, the latter of which is crucial for school success. Working-class children, through their socialization in position-oriented families, have limited access to an elaborated code, and so do poorly in school. This is an enormous simplification of his very elaborate argument but is nevertheless the gist of the matter. Bernstein has been widely misunderstood in the United States, where his work has been totally inappropriately applied to Black children.

We see, then, that the use of sociolinguistic theory tends to be problem-oriented in its applications, frequently dealing with the language learning difficulties children from other than mainstream groups experience in our schools.

Sociolinguistic Situations

Sociolinguistic situations are the real-world situations in which the students are going to use their English; this brings up the question of defining the objectives of language teaching in terms of the functions of these needs. English for Special Purposes and English for Science and Technology have been major developments during the last decade in ESL (Lackstrom et al. 1970; Richards 1976; Selinker et al. 1972).

Sociolinguistic Description

This is the area where I think the most interesting work has been done in ESL during the last ten years, but then that may be a biased opinion. Still, my guess is that twenty years from now, when the Silent Way and Suggestopedia are gone, we will still use the sociolinguistic descriptions of speech acts, discourse, and cross-cultural communication which now surface in our journals.

Dell Hymes, the anthropological linguist, has suggested that linguistic competence is not sufficient for an adequate description of language, which must also take into account when, how, and to whom it is appropriate to speak; that is, a "communicative competence" (Hymes 1967; 1972a; 1972b; 1972c; 1974), or in Grimshaw's terms "the systemic sets of social interactional rules" (1973:109). More than any other single concept, the notion of communicative competence has influenced our thinking about teaching ESL. There are two major approaches within ESL at present, and one of them is a communicative approach to language teaching (Brumfit and Johnson 1979; Canale and Swain 1979; Candlin 1975; Munby 1978; Roulet and Holec 1976; Widdowson 1978; Wilkins 1976). Such an approach argues that the focus of language teaching should be on language use, rather than form, although most scholars consider linguistic competence to be part of communicative competence. The discrete units or teaching points of a lesson, syllabus, or textbook then cease being grammatical patterns, sequenced in an orderly manner, and instead become speech acts[2] or in Wilkins' terms

---

[2] Speech act is a difficult concept to define; Austin (1962) and Searle (1969) have written books to do so. Hymes defines a "speech act," like a joke, as the minimal term of the set "speech event," a conversation, and "speech situation," a party (1972a: 56). Not that teaching speech acts is new. Kelly (1969) discusses the teaching of phrases of social life, like courting, social calls,

"notions" and "functions." Not that there is total agreement on this manner of organizing textbooks. In one of the latest issues of Applied Linguistics (1981, 2:1), both Brumfit and I argue against a purely functional approach in syllabus construction where the main argument is, I think, that language forms are generative while functions are not. One can, of course, (and, I would add, should) combine form and function in one's teaching.

Johnson and Morrow's Communicate (1978) and Approaches (1979) were two of the first textbooks to adhere to a functional approach. Today it is a publisher's darling. A number of journal articles tackle the problem of speech act description (Borkin and Reinhart 1978; Carrell and Konneker 1981; Ervin-Tripp 1976; Levinson 1980; Rintell 1979; Scarcella 1979; Walters 1979; Wolfson 1981). Interestingly enough, sociolinguistics rated very high, right up with phonetics, on the questionnaire the ELI instructors had been asked to answer about the usefulness of linguistics for language teaching. All of them singled out speech act theory as helpful. I think this somewhat surprising response reflects the fact that although our culture rules and ways of doing things permeate our life, we are rarely aware of those rules until they are broken. It is difficult to talk about and teach cultural rules without any training. Several instructors commented that such study had given them a way of systematically organizing the data and a metalanguage--which they avoided using in the classroom--to think about such phenomena. One instructor added that such understanding also allowed her to know exactly what questions to ask in the classroom in order to bring out a kind of cultural contrastive analysis of speech acts. A compliment in Japanese is not necessarily one in English (Wolfson 1981), and students need to be made aware of that.

Finally, ESL teachers are sensitive to their students as human beings. In the words of one instructor: "Sociolinguistics has helped me become aware of different cultural norms and possible differences, perhaps more importantly.... It helps in dealing with the students on a personal level."

---

and quarreling during the Renaissance, Shakespeare even satirized lessons from Florio. There is very little new in language teaching, except maybe the Silent Way.

Linguistic Theory and Descriptions of Languages

Back in 1969, Wardhaugh wrote a TESOL State of the Art paper in which he outlined the tenets of transformational-generative grammar and commented on the insights into language it gave. He concluded: "However, neither the grammar nor existing descriptions give teachers any way of teaching these insights nor do they provide any way of assigning a truth value to the insights on an absolute scale, apparent claims to the contrary notwithstanding" (1969:12). I think Wardhaugh's remark still stands. The most intelligent statement of the value TG grammar for language teaching was Robin Lakoff's "Transformation Grammar and Language Teaching" (1969), and she has since retracted her words, saying she was simply mistaken (1974). Rutherford's Modern English (1968), for which claims were made that it followed a TG approach, in its second edition reflects a change toward more traditional grammar. In fact, we tend to find the same absence of overt linguistics in textbooks as I found in classroom observation. Furey (1972) found, in an analysis of the grammatical rules and explanations, very little difference in textbooks of respectively audio-lingual, direct method, TG, and eclectic orientation. Presumably this is so, she says, because of the pedagogical necessity of simplifications of rules.

There are, of course, linguistic theories other than TG grammar, such as case grammar (Nilsen 1971) and tagmemics (Paulston 1970), which are used for ESL purposes. The trouble is that few ESL teachers today are trained in structural linguistics, which I maintain is much more suitable for pedagogical purposes. In fact, the eclectic approach exemplified by Quirk and Greenbaum (1973) and Quirk, Greenbaum, Leech and Svartvik (1972) is the generally prevailing approach in language teaching.

My view that theoretical linguistics has lacked any influence on language teaching during the last decade needs to be modified. Chomsky undeniably changed the climate of linguistic thought in the United States. Chomsky's attack of language acquisition as habit formation has had enormous consequences in our thinking about language teaching. Language learning as a creative act is the basic foundation of most present-day ESL methods and is one source for our interest in error analysis.

The way teachers deal with errors in the classroom is closely influenced by their linguistic knowledge.

Experienced teachers tend to correct what they judge to be performance errors with a reference to the rule, and so elicit the correction from the student himself. On the other hand, a competence error repeated by several students will bring on a modelling by the teacher of the grammatical pattern, sometimes in a contrast to other familiar patterns, and a grammatical explanation of its function. I saw this repeated several times in my class observations. Thinking on one's feet and being able to come up with good example sentences is in fact what one instructor cites as the major benefit of her syntax course. Most instructors agree that Standard Theory syntax is too abstract to be of much use in the classroom, but they cite as very useful in their teaching the insight into: <u>patterns</u> of English, knowing what is rule-governed <u>behavior</u> and what needs to be memorized, what structures are similar and different, and knowing what goes together. One of them writes: "Since I've studied linguistics I've become <u>more</u> convinced of the notion that language has a <u>definite</u> structure/system, which means I now no longer feel quite so helpless about teaching grammar." The last point is important. It became very clear in the interviews that teachers dislike intensely to feel ignorant or uncertain about what they are teaching, and that they worry about their explanations and presentation of teaching points. The study of linguistics brings them confidence and security, and they are very conscious about that relationship.

The instructors are unanimous in their opinion that phonetics is most useful. It is the only coursework that ranks higher than sociolinguistics. The reason is simple: "I understand how the sounds are articulated and can tell the students." It also develops their ear so they can hear and know what the students do wrong. They find basic concepts in phonemics useful, but most reject generative phonology. Surprisingly, many also reject grammatical analysis, morphology, and field methods, and less surprisingly, historical linguistics and Montague grammar. They all consider linguistic structures of English, in which they use Quirk and Greenbaum (1973), as basically boring but nevertheless essential.

We see, then, that even if I have doubt about the usefulness of present-day linguistics for language teaching, our students do not. Even if they consider only two courses in linguistic theory, phonetics and English grammar, as core courses, they insist that the study of syntax brings them a <u>Weltanschauung</u>, or worldview, of language which they <u>find eminently</u> useful.

Defining Content Items

By this term, Roulet means the selection and sequencing of language materials for the curriculum or textbook. Structural linguists gave a lot of thought and energy to the optimum selection and sequencing of language items, but these days this is an unfashionable topic. The occasional argument is rather whether one should teach function before form, and of course there is the notional-functional argument that syllabi should be organized on the basis of communicative functions rather than on grammatical patterns.[3] As Canale and Swain (1979:58) point out, there are no empirical data on the relative effectiveness or ineffectiveness of either approach.

Psycholinguistic Theory

In 1969 Wardhaugh predicted that cognitive psychology would influence language teaching for many years to come, and thus far his prediction holds. Ausubel (1968) is still frequently cited in footnotes, everyone insists language learning must be meaningful, the notion of language learning as habit formation is dismissed, and there seems to be a general consensus that grammatical rules and explanations are beneficial for adults.

Besides cognitive psychology, psycholinguistics (Clark and Clark 1977; Dato 1975; Slobin 1971; Taylor 1976) and neurolinguistics (Albert and Obler 1978; Lenneberg and Lenneberg 1975; Rieber 1976) are topics of recent interest. Especially in regard to neurolinguistics, caution is needed in drawing implications for the classroom. At this point I think it is safe to say that the evidence (from aphasia, split brain operations, dichotic listening tests, etc.) indicates that individuals have different ways of learning, for which there may be a biological foundation. But that was known before. I find the readings in neurolinguistics the most interesting in the language learning field today. But I worry about premature applications, and I react against the fads which claim to draw on neurolinguistics.

In psycholinguistics, there has been much L_2 acquisition research during the last decade. Douglas

---

[3]Actually, I have never seen a clear definition of what _notion_ means, and most writers in fact settle for functions which I take to be similar to speech acts, getting things done with words.

Brown, in an editorial in Language Learning in 1974, comments on the "new wave" of research: "For perhaps the first time in history, L_2 research is characterized by a rigorous empirical approach coupled with cautious rationalism" and goes on to claim that "the results of current L_2 research will indeed have a great impact on shaping a new method" (1974:v-vi). This has not happened, and it is still too early to see what the implications will be.

It is difficult to single out any specific studies, but the best place to begin is probably with Roger Brown's A First Language (1973). Along with his basic finding that "there is an approximately invariant order to acquisition for the 14 morphemes we have studied, and behind this invariance lies not modeling frequency but semantic and grammatical complexity" (1973: 379) (a finding supported by the L_2 studies), he also carefully investigates the psychological reality of TG transformational rules, a notion he is forced to reject as invalid. Instead he posits the concept of semantic saliency, a notion which may hold direct implications for language teaching.

Whatever the implications for language teaching which we will eventually draw from this "new wave" of L_2 acquisition research, Brown is right in pointing out a major significance, the turning to empirical evidence rather than to unsubstantiated claims and counterclaims.

The greatest surprises of the questionnaire responses were to be found in the TAs' reactions to psycholinguistic theory. They held it to be of marginal utility. I will quote one instructor at length.

> Nothing very directly applicable; but by increasing my knowledge of the mental processes involved in language use (well, at least of people's theories about them), it's increased my...my what? I think this is a case where I have to resort to a general "the more I know about language and language learning, the better teacher I'll be." The most pertinent research (in reading, L_1 acquisition, etc.) seems better at pointing out what variables are probably insignificant than at telling us which ones are important.

I think this attitude reflects the fact that we really don't know how people learn language.

Descriptions of learning strategies and models of performance

Theory of Language Pedagogy

A thorough exploration of these two topics would require a book or two to complete and would take us too far afield for the purposes of this paper. The audiolingual method drew heavily on linguistics in its development. Today that method has been discredited, maybe at times unfairly, as it is blamed for infelicities which Fries certainly never intended. A careful reading of his <u>Teaching and Learning English as a Foreign Language</u> (1945) will reveal it as sensible a book today as the day it was written.

In today's thinking about language teaching, psychology seems to play a larger part than linguistics. "Cognitive code" (John Carroll's term) is recognized as a general trend, with its emphasis on meaningful learning and careful analysis of linguistic structures. The cognitive code approach can be considered a reaction against the audiolingual, both from theoretical and practical viewpoints. The approach closely reflects the transformational-generative linguistic school of thought about the nature of language, and it is influenced by cognitive psychologists, critical of stimulus-reinforcement theory, such as Ausubel (1958). It holds that language is a rule-governed, creative system of a universal nature. Language learning must be meaningful, rote-learning should be avoided, and the primary emphasis is on analysis and developing competence, in Chomsky's sense of the word. We see the same nice fit between linguistic theory and psychological theory in cognitive code methodology we once had in the audiolingual method. The trouble with cognitive code is that I know of not one single textbook for beginning students which can be classified as strict cognitive code.

In practical fact, most language teaching specialists are eclectic, and so are the textbooks they write. Carroll (1974) holds that there is nothing mutually exclusive in the theories of Skinner and of Lenneberg-Chomsky about language learning, but rather that these theories are complementary. This opinion is reflected in the eclectic approach to methodology which is characteristic of most of the methods texts at the technique level. Most of the writers of these texts agree that all four skills--listening, speaking, reading and writing--should be introduced simultaneously without undue postponement of any one. The importance of writing as a service activity for the other skills is generally recognized, and there is considerable interest in controlled composition. No one talks any longer about memorizing long dialogues. Listening comprehension is still poorly understood on a theoretical level, but there is more emphasis on the teaching of that skill. The crucial importance of vocabulary, the ignoring of which was one of the worse faults of the audiolingual approach, is increasingly gaining acceptance.

I think we agree with Chastain that "perhaps too much attention has been given to proper pronunciation" (1976), and we now tend to think that it is more important that the learner can communicate his ideas than that he can practice utterances with perfect pronunciation. The one thing that everyone is absolutely certain about is the necessity to use language for communicative purposes in the classroom. As early as 1968, Oller and Obrecht concluded from an experiment that communicative activity should be a central point of pattern drills from the very first stages of language learning. Savignon's (1971) widely-cited dissertation confirmed that beyond doubt. Many bridle at pattern drills, but it is not very important because we agree on the basic principle of meaningful learning for the purpose of communication. And that basic principle is indicative of what may be the most significant trend: our increasing concentration on our students' learning rather than on our teaching (Oller and Richards, 1973).

In addition to the prevailing eclecticism, several new methods have gained visibility recently in the United States. In alphabetical order they are: Community Counseling Learning, Rapid Acquisition, the Silent Way, Suggestopedia, and Total Physical Response.[4]

Community Counseling Learning or Community Language Learning (CLL) was developed by Charles A. Curran (1976) from his earlier work in affective psychology. In CLL the students sit in a circle with a tape recorder and talk about whatever interests them. The teacher, whose role is seen as a counselor, serves as a resource person rather than as a traditional "teacher." At the very beginning stages, the counselor also serves

---

[4] Maybe the Monitor Model should be mentioned here too, but at this point it is a theoretical model of language learning rather than a method for language teaching.

as translator for his clients: the students first utter in their native language, the teacher translates, and the students repeat their own utterances in the L_2. The tape is played back, errors analyzed and the clients copy down whatever structures they need to work on. Adherents of this method tend to be ardent in their fervor as they point out that this method teaches "the whole person" within a supportive community which minimizes the risk-taking held necessary for language learning. Another value of this method lies in the motivational aspect in that students can talk about issues of concern to them (Stevick 1976; 1980).

"Rapid Acquisition of a Foreign Language by Avoidance of Speaking" is an approach developed by Winitz and Reeds (1973). The authors believe that there is a natural sequence (neurological) in language learning, and they stress that listening comprehension should be complete before students are allowed to speak. Length of utterance is limited, problem-solving through the use of pictures is stressed, and the syllabus is limited to base structures and limited vocabulary.

The Silent Way was developed by Caleb Gattegno in 1963 but not published here until 1972. In the Silent Way, the teacher uses Cuisinière rods, a color-coded wall chart for pronunciation, and speaks each new word only once; the responsibility for learning and talking is shifted to the students. Even correction is handled through gestures and mime by the teacher, with no further modeling. Many teachers are enthusiastic about this method, but I have also many anecdotes of student rebellion (Stevick 1980).

Suggestopedia, a method developed by Georgi Lozanov at the Institute of Suggestology in Sofia, Bulgaria (Bancroft 1978; Lozanov 1979) claims to reduce the stress of language learning. Listening and speaking are stressed, with emphasis on vocabulary acquisition. The Suggestopedic Cycle begins with review of previously learned material in the target language, followed by introduction of new material. This is followed by a one-hour seance during which students listen to the new material against a background of baroque music. The students also do breathing exercises and yoga relaxation techniques which are said to increase concentration and tap the powers of the subconscious. There is also considerable roleplay of real-life situations.

Total Physical Response, developed by James Asher (1969; cf. Asher and Adamski 1977), also stresses listening comprehension as he believes that if listening and speaking are introduced simultaneously, listening comprehension is much delayed. Basically the method consists of having students listen to commands and then carry them out.

I refrain from commenting on these methods, since it is not my opinion that is important but rather the teacher's. As long as teacher <u>and students</u> have confidence that they are in fact <u>learning, and all</u> are happy in the process, I don't think the methods make that much difference.

In conclusion, we can say that Newmark, after all, is more right than Chomsky about the significance of linguistics for the teaching of languages. But Chomsky is right, too, for that influence is not immediately apparent. Linguistics is like our proverbial bottom of the iceberg, mostly invisible, but massively giving shape and direction to the teaching. It took me several hours of reflection to realize that I had not heard any incorrect grammatical explanation, which was also an indication of linguistics at work.

Most of all, linguistics becomes a worldview. It colors the approach to language, the recognition of problems, and the attempts to find solutions. Our TA's rejection of a formal approach to the passive construction, characteristic of a structural approach to linguistics, would once have been branded as mentalism, but reflects what may be the most important contribution of present-day linguistics: a different attitude towards language.

References

Abrahams, Roger and Rudolph Troike. 1972. *Language and cultural diversity in American education*. Englewood Cliffs, N. J.: Prentice-Hall.

Albert, Martin L. and Loraine K. Obler. 1978. *The bilingual brain: Neuropsychological and neurolinguistic aspects of bilingualism*. New York: Academic Press.

Allen, John P. B. and S. Pit Corder (eds.). 1975. *Papers in applied linguistics*. London: Oxford University Press.

Asher, J. 1969. The total physical response approach to second language learning. *Modern Language Learning* 53:1.3-17.

────── and C. Adamski. 1977. *Learning another language through actions: The complete teacher's guidebook*. Los Gatos, Calif.: Sky Oak Productions.

Austin, John L. 1962. *How to do things with words*. Cambridge, Mass.: Harvard University Press.

Ausubel, David P. 1968. *Educational psychology: A cognitive view*. New York: Holt, Rinehart and Winston.

Bancroft, W. J. 1978. The Lozanov method and its American adaptations. *Modern Language Journal* 62:4. 167-74.

Baratz, Joan C. and Roger W. Shuy. 1969. *Teaching black children to read*. Washington, D. C.: Center for Applied Linguistics.

Bereiter, Carl and S. Engelmann. 1966. *Teaching disadvantaged children in the preschool*. Englewood Cliffs, N. J.: Prentice-Hall.

Bernstein, Basil. 1971. *Class, codes and control*, Vol. 1: Theoretical studies towards a sociology of language. London: Routledge and Kegan Paul.

──────. 1972. A Sociolinguistic Approach to Socialization; with some reference to educability. In John J. Gumperz and Dell Hymes (eds.), *Directions in Sociolinguistics*. New York: Holt, Rinehart and Winston.

———. 1973. *Class, codes and control*, Vol 2. London: Routledge and Kegan Paul.

Borkin, Ann and Susan M. Reinhart. 1978. Excuse me and I'm sorry. *TESOL Quarterly* 12.57-70.

Brown, H. Douglas. 1974. (editorial) *Language Learning* 24:2, pp. v-vi.

Brown, Roger W. 1973. *A first language: The early stages*. Cambridge, Mass.: Harvard University Press.

Brumfit, Christopher J. 1981. Notional syllabuses revisited: A response. *Applied Linguistics* 2:1.90-92.

——— and K. Johnson (eds.). 1980. *The communicative approach to language teaching*. Oxford: Oxford University Press.

Burger, H. 1971. *Ethno-pedagogy: Cross-cultural teaching techniques*. Albuquerque, N. M.: Southwestern Cooperative Educational Laboratory.

Canale, M. and M. Swain. 1979. *Communicative approaches to second language teaching and testing*. Ontario: Ministry of Education.

Candlin, C. (ed.) 1975. *The communicative teaching of English*. London: Longman.

Carrell, Patricia L. and Beverly H. Konneker. 1981. Politeness: comparing native and nonnative judgments. *Language Learning* 31.17-30.

Carroll, John B. 1974. Learning theory for the classroom teacher. In Gilbert A. Jarvis (ed.), *The challenge of communication*. Skokie, Ill.: National Textbook Company.

Cazden, Courtney B., Vera P. John, and Dell Hymes (eds.). 1972. *Functions of language in the classroom*. New York: Teachers College Press, Columbia University.

Chastain, Kenneth. 1976. *Developing second language skills: Theory to practice*. 2nd ed. Chicago: Rand, McNally.

Chomsky, Noam. 1966. Linguistic theory. *Language Teaching: Broader contexts*. Northeast Conference on the Teaching of Foreign Languages.

Clark, Herbert H. and Eve V. Clark. 1977. *Psychology and language*. New York: Harcourt Brace Jovanovich.

Corder, S. Pit. 1973. *Introducing applied linguistics*. Baltimore: Penguin Books.

———. 1975. Applied linguistics and language teaching. In John P. B. Allen and S. Pit Corder (eds.), Papers in applied linguistics. London: Oxford University Press.

Curran, Charles A. 1976. Counseling-learning in second languages. Apple River, Ill.: Apple River Press.

Dato, Daniel P. (ed.). 1975. Developmental psycholinguistics: theory and applications. Georgetown University Round Table on Languages and Linguistics. Washington, D. C.: Georgetown University Press.

Dillard, Joey L. 1972. Black English: Its history and usage in the United States. New York: Vintage Books.

Ervin-Tripp, S. 1976. Is Sybil there? The structure of some American English directives. Language in Society 5.25-66.

Fasold, Ralph W. and Roger W. Shuy (eds.). 1970. Teaching standard English in the inner city. Washington, D. C.: Center for Applied Linguistics.

Feigenbaum, Irwin. 1970. The use of nonstandard English in teaching standard: contrast and comparison. In Fasold and Shuy (eds.).

Fries, Charles C. 1945. Teaching and learning English as a foreign language. Ann Arbor, Mich.: University of Michigan Press.

Furey, P. 1972. Grammar explanations in foreign language teaching. Unpublished MA thesis, University of Pittsburgh.

Gattegno, Caleb. 1972. Teaching foreign languages in schools: The silent way. 2nd ed. New York: Educational Solutions.

Gleason, Henry A., Jr. 1955. An introduction to descriptive linguistics. New York: Holt, Rinehart and Winston.

Grimshaw, Allen D. 1973. Rules, social interaction, and language behavior. TESOL Quarterly 7.99-115.

Hymes, Dell H. 1967. The anthropology of communication. In F. Dance (ed.), Human communication theory, New York: Holt, Rinehart and Winston.

———. 1972a. Models of the interaction of language and social life. In John Gumperz and Dell Hymes (eds.), Directions in sociolinguistics. New York: Holt, Rinehart and Winston.

———. 1972b. Introduction. In Courtney Cazden, Vera John and Dell Hymes (eds.), The function of language in the classroom. New York: Teachers College Press, pp. xi-lviii.

———. 1972c. On communicative competence. In J. B. Pride and J. Holmes (eds.), Sociolinguistics. Harmondsworth, England: Penguin Books, pp. 269-293.

———. 1974. Foundations in sociolinguistics: An Ethnographic approach. Philadelphia: University of Pennsylvania Press.

Jensen, A. 1969. How much can we boost I. Q. and scholastic achievement? Harvard Educational Review 39.1.

Johnson, K. and K. Morrow. 1978. Communicate. Reading: University of Reading.

——— and ———. 1979. Approaches. Cambridge: Cambridge University Press.

Kelly, Louis G. 1969. Twenty-five centuries of language teaching. Rowley, Mass.: Newbury House.

Kochman, Thomas E. (ed.). 1972. Rappin' and stylin' out: Communication in urban Black America. Chicago: University of Illinois Press.

Krashen, S. D. 1972. The monitor model for adult second language performance. In Marina Burt, Heidi Dulay, and Mary Finocchiaro (eds.), Viewpoints on English as a second language. New York: Regents.

Labov, William. 1969. The study of non-standard English. Washington, D. C.: ERIC, Center for Applied Linguistics.

Lackstrom, John E., Larry Selinker and Louis P. Trimble. 1970. "Grammar and Technical English." In Robert C. Lugton (ed.), English as a second language: Current issues. Chilton Press.

Lado, Robert. 1957. Linguistics across cultures: Applied linguistics for language teachers. Ann Arbor: University of Michigan Press.

Lakoff, Robin. 1969. Transformational grammar and language teaching. Language Learning, 19:117-140.

———. 1974. Linguistic theory and the real world. Paper presented at the TESOL Convention 1974, Denver, Colorado.

Larsen-Freeman, Diane. 1981. The 'What' of second language acquisition. In M. Hines, and W. Rutherford, (eds.), On TESOL '81, Washington, D. C., TESOL.

Lenneberg, Eric H. and Elizabeth H. Lenneberg, (eds.). 1975. Foundations of Language Development: A multidisciplinary approach. New York: Academic Press.

Levinson, S. 1980. Speech act theory: "The state of the art." Language teaching and linguistic abstracts 13.5-24.

Lozanov, Georgi. 1978. Suggestology and outlines of suggestopedy. New York: Gordon and Breach.

Mitchell-Kernan, Claudia. 1971. Language behavior in a black urban community. Monographs of the Language-Behavior Research Laboratory No. 2, University of California at Berkeley.

Moulton, William G. 1961. Linguistics and language teaching in the United States: 1940-1960. In Christine Mohrmann, Alf Sommerfelt and Joshua Whatwaugh (eds.), Trends in European and American linguistics: 1930-1960. Utrecht: Spectrum.

———. 1970. Linguistic guide to language learning, 2nd ed. New York: Modern Language Association.

Munby, J. 1978. Communicative syllabus design. Cambridge: Cambridge University Press.

Newmark, Leonard. 1970. Grammatical theory and the teaching of English as a foreign language. In Mark Lester (ed.), Readings in applied transformational grammar. New York: Holt, Rinehart and Winston.

Nida, Eugene A. 1949. Morphology: The descriptive analysis of words. Ann Arbor: University of Michigan Press.

———. 1954. Customs and cultures. New York: Harper.

Nilsen, Don L. F. 1971. The use of case grammar in teaching English as a foreign language. TESOL Quarterly, 5:4.293-300.

Norris, W. 1972. TESOL at the beginning of the '70s: Trends, topics, and research needs. Pittsburgh, PA: University Center for International Studies.

Oller, John W., Jr. and Dean H. Obrecht. 1968. Pattern drill and communicative activity: A psycholinguistic experiment. IRAL 6:2.165-174.

——— and Jack C. Richards (eds.). 1973. Focus on the learner: Pragmatic perspectives for the language teacher. Rowley, Mass.: Newbury House.

Paulston, C. B. 1970. Teaching footnotes and bibliographical entries to foreign students: A tagmemic approach. English Language Teaching. 34.3.

———. 1981. Notional syllabuses revisited: Some comments. Applied Linguistics 2:1.93-95.

Pike, Kenneth. 1947. Phonemics: A technique for reducing languages to writing. Ann Arbor: University of Michigan Press.

Quirk, Randolph and Sidney Greenbaum. 1973. A concise grammar of contemporary English. New York: Harcourt Brace Jovanovich.

———, ———, G. Leech, and Jan Svartvik. 1972. A grammar of contemporary English. New York: Seminar Press.

Richards, Jack C. 1974. Error analysis: Perspectives on second language acquisition. London: Longman.

———. 1976. Teaching English for science and technology. Singapore: RELC.

Rieber, Robert W. (ed.). 1976. The Neuropsychology of Language. New York: Plenum Press.

Rintell, Ellen. 1979. Getting your speech act together: The pragmatic ability of second language learners. Working Papers on Bilingualism 17.97-106.

Roulet, E. 1975. Linguistic theory, linguistic description, and language teaching. London: Longman.

——— and Holec. 1976. L'enseignement de la competence de communication en langues secondes. Neuchatel: Université de Neuchatel.

Rutherford, William E. 1968. Modern English., Vol 1. New York: Harcourt, Brace & World. (2nd ed., paper, 1975).

Savignon, S. 1971. Study of the effect of training in communicative skills as part of a beginning college French course on student attitude and achievement in linguistic and communicative competence. Ph. D. dissertation, University of Illinois at Urbana-Champaign.

Saville-Troike, Muriel. 1976. Foundations for Teaching English as a Second Language: Theory and Method for Multicultural Education. Englewood Cliffs, N. J.: Prentice-Hall.

Scarcella, R. 1979. On speaking politely in a second language. In C. Yorio, K. Perkins, and J. Schacter (eds.), On TESOL '79, Washington, D. C.: TESOL.

Schachter, Jacquelyn. 1974. An error in error analysis, Language Learning, 24:2.205-214.

Searle, J. 1969. A classification of illocutionary acts. Language in Society 5.1-25.

Selinker, Larry, Louis Trimble, and Robert Vroman. 1971. Working papers in English for science and technology. Seattle: University of Washington, College of Engineering.

Slobin, Dan I. 1971. Psycholinguistics. Glenview, Ill.: Scott, Foresman & Co.

Spolsky, B. 1969. Linguistics and language pedagogy-- Applications or implications? In Georgetown University Round Table Monograph Series on Languages and Linguistics 22.143-156.

———. 1978. Educational linguistics: An introduction. Rowley, Mass.: Newbury House.

Stevick, Earl. 1976. Memory, meaning and method: Some Psychological perspectives on language learning. Rowley, Mass.: Newbury House.

———. 1980. Teaching languages: A way and ways. Rowley, Mass.: Newbury House.

Taylor, Insup. 1976. Introduction to psycholinguistics. New York: Holt, Rinehart and Winston.

Trueba, Henry T. and Carol Barnett-Migrahi (eds.). 1979. Bilingual multicultural education and the professional. Rowley, Mass.: Newbury House.

Van Ek, J. A. 1978. The threshold level for modern language learning in schools. Longmans.

Walters, Joel. 1979. Strategies for requesting in Spanish and English. Language Learning 29.277-293.

Wardhaugh, Ronald. 1969. Teaching English to speakers of other languages: the state of the art. Washington, D. C.: ERIC, Center for Applied Linguistics, ED 030119.

Warriner, J. E., M. E. Whitten, and F. Griffith. 1975. English grammar and composition. New York: Harcourt, Brace, Jovanovich.

Widdowson, H. G. 1978. *Teaching language as communication*. London: Oxford University Press.

Wilkins, D. A. 1977. *Notional syllabuses*. Oxford: Oxford University Press.

Winitz, Harris and James A. Reeds. 1973. Rapid acquisition of a foreign language (German) by the avoidance of speaking. *IRAL* 11:4.295-317.

Wolfram, Walter A. 1969. *A sociolinguistic description of Detroit Negro speech*. Washington, D. C.: Center for Applied Linguistics.

────── and Nona Clarke (eds.). 1971. *Black-white speech relationships*. Washington, D. C.: Center for Applied Linguistics.

Wolfson, Nessa. 1981. Compliments in cross-cultural perspective. *TESOL Quarterly* 15:2.117-124.

www.ingramcontent.com/pod-product-compliance
Lightning Source LLC
Chambersburg PA
CBHW072219240426
43670CB00038B/2367